Burnley

Burnley

The Glory Years Remembered

Mike Prestage

The Breedon Books
Publishing Company
Derby

First published in Great Britain in 2000 by
The Breedon Books Publishing Company Limited
Breedon House, 3 The Parker Centre, Derby, DE21 4SZ.

ISBN 1 85983 200 8

Printed and bound by Butler & Tanner Ltd., Selwood Printing Works,
Caxton Road, Frome, Somerset.

Colour separations and jacket printing by
GreenShires Group Ltd., Leicester.

Contents

Acknowledgements

To all the ex-players and
long-time supporters of Burnley
Football Club who took the time
to share their memories.

Introduction

IN THE Fifties, Burnley Football Club set about producing one of the finest English club sides of the 20th century. The name of this club from the small Lancashire mill town was mentioned in the same breath as the glamour clubs of Manchester United, Arsenal and Tottenham Hotspur, and for a while Burnley FC were the cotton town kings of football.

This story, though, begins at the start of a remarkable era when the end of World War Two saw football emerge as the leisure escape of the masses. In these glory years, forty million people a season poured through the turnstiles to watch League soccer. Today, for all the hype surrounding the Premiership, the number of paying fans is half that.

The industrial towns of Lancashire were at the forefront of this football boom. And for a time, towards its end, Burnley were the most successful. The club were aided by the maximum wage, which meant there was no financial advantage in players moving clubs. They also had an innovative youth policy and a finely-honed scouting system that was particularly effective in the North East. It saw the emergence in the late Fifties and early Sixties of a side that were League champions in 1959-60, and in 1961-62 they came within two matches of winning what was then the 'Holy Grail' of English football – the Football League and FA Cup Double.

There was earlier success, though. When League football resumed after the war, Burnley were in the Second Division. They did not stay there long, however, and that first post-war season of 1946-47 saw them win promotion and reach the FA Cup Final, where they were cruelly beaten 1-0 after extra-time by Charlton Athletic. With their famous 'Iron Curtain' defence that set new records for the least goals conceded in a season, Burnley began this new era with a team that was a match for anyone.

George Bray had joined Burnley from Great Harwood Town in October 1937, made his League début the following year at left-half and was part of the great Burnley side of the Forties. For him, the post-war years were special because the war had robbed him of six years of his career and starved the public of League football. He explained that he hadn't even had the chance of wartime professional football, guesting for a club close to where he was stationed. His commanding officer was keen to keep the best players for the regiment team. It meant he played a lower standard for nothing, rather than pick up thirty shillings for turning out for Burnley or guesting for another League club.

He said: "I did my share in the army in the war. I had just got into the first team at Burnley when war broke out and it cost me some of my best years. When it was all over, we just wanted to get back playing and resume our careers. Everybody wanted to put what we had all been through behind us. Those early seasons were wonderful. Football was just at the top and Burnley were quickly being recognised as a good club. We got back into the First Division at the first attempt and had a good side. After the break, I was pleased to be back into training and I don't think I did too bad."

Not only did Bray not do too bad, he would be a first choice until 1951 when, at the age of 32, he played his last game. The arrival of one Jimmy Adamson ensured a shuffle in the ranks that saw Reg Attwell switch from the right to take Bray's left-half berth, to make room for the young prodigy. Bray joined the backroom staff at Turf Moor where he remained for more than fifty years as a popular trainer. Now in his eighties, he is still an enthusiastic supporter of Burnley Football Club.

He adds: "In those days the football team put the town of Burnley on the map and gave everybody something to be proud of. There was nothing much happening in Burnley, but when we got to Wembley, that made everybody sit up and take notice. It is a little town, but once we got promotion it meant all the big clubs would be coming here to play. Everybody in the town loved that."

Bray adds, though, that the maximum wage ensured there was not a fortune to be made in the game for a professional footballer. In theory he could be on the same money as an international he was playing against or alongside. However, he reveals he is not wholly convinced that this was actually the case. "Nobody was on the sort of money players earn nowadays, but I think there was some cheating on the maximum wage, although nobody knew for sure. It seemed that everybody was getting the same money, but it didn't happen. There was always somebody who cooked the books. We could at least all rely on the Professional Footballers' Association. We had a good union to look after us. When a footballer finished, he seemed to go out of existence, but at least the union was there if needed. If a player had been with the club five years, he got a benefit, which could raise between £500 and £650 – and then that was it."

Despite the money not securing a player's financial future as it does today, Bray still has fond memories of his time in football and with Burnley, where he spent his entire professional career. "Football has given me a good life and I'm very thankful. I have had some good times, especially the run up to Wembley which is the dream of everybody who has been in football. I would never run football down. It's hard and you need a bit of luck to get the break, but if you make the grade, it's wonderful. I enjoyed every minute of my career and if I had my time again I wouldn't change a thing."

Burnley have always managed to generate fanatical support, not just in the good times but also after the Clarets' slide down the divisions when they could still rely on attendances far in excess of their rivals. The arrival of former England and Arsenal striker Ian Wright during the 1999-2000 season saw more than 20,000 supporters at Turf Moor to watch Second Division football. It was a remarkable achievement and proof that, given something to cheer, the people of Burnley will rally to the Claret and Blue cause.

The town, like its football team, may have fallen on hard times in recent years, but there is still a firmly held conviction among the locals that both will enjoy better fortunes again. Winning promotion to Division One in the first season of the new millennium is just the beginning. And while talk of the Premiership may be on the optimistic side at present, it cannot now be laughingly dismissed as it might have been a season or two ago. Who knows, Burnley FC may yet reclaim their place in the elite, a place that many of a certain age regard as a birthright.

Alastair Campbell, Prime Minister Tony Blair's Downing Street spokesman and key adviser, is a lifelong Burnley fan and has seen the best of times and the worst of times following the side. Writing in *The Observer* newspaper, he captured the spirit of the club and its supporters when he wrote: "Go to Burnley on match days and you know there's a game on. We get bigger crowds per head of local population than any club in the country, possibly the world (Manchester United would need about 300,000 a game to get near us, or so we tell each other). And go to parks and playgrounds in the town... if kids are wearing strips, they're Burnley strips, not Man U or Arsenal, like in most playgrounds. There is a passion for the club that few can match. Ask all the former players who have settled there and go back every week."

The measure of the depth of support can be gauged, he believes, by a question that will baffle many at pub quiz nights – although not, of course, if the event is being staged within the old mill town's borders. When was the last time the Wembley crowd topped 80,000? The answer is the 1988 Sherpa Van Final when Burnley met Wolves, a game Burnley lost 2-0. As Campbell wryly notes, the highlight for the Burnley fans was the teams running out on to the Wembley pitch. As so often for the fans in recent years, the high was quickly followed by a depressing low.

Although he saw the great side of the early Sixties, he was too young to recall seeing the legendary names in action. "I was apparently at the final games of Jimmy McIlroy, reckoned to be the greatest player ever to wear claret and blue, and Jimmy Adamson, still one of just two uncapped Footballers of the Year (the other is Tony Book). Older fans say that hearing McIlroy was going to Stoke was one of those 'where were you when...' moments, on a par with moon landings and presidential assassinations, so it is a cause of shame and regret that I have no recollection of him playing. Likewise with Adamson. On sleepless nights I urge my memory to throw up just a flash of him running with the ball at his feet, but to no avail."

He said that such has been the fall in Burnley's playing fortunes that there are fans who are not only members of the 92 Club, having been to every League club ground, but who have seen Burnley play at them all. And the club boasts, along with Wolverhampton Wanderers, of being the only side to have won all four divisional championships.

Peter and Christine Marsden are among Burnley's most devoted fans and are among that band who have been to all 92 League grounds following the Clarets. Peter has not missed a game since the late Sixties. Christine keeps her own records and a photograph collection of players and grounds. For them supporting Burnley has become an obsession and they never miss a match. Peter recalls: "I started going in the early Sixties. My dad wasn't that keen, but he got a friend of the family to take me and I have been hooked ever since. We used to walk to the ground with excitement mounting as we got nearer. The Sixties team was brilliant. There were so many good players."

Tommy Cummings remembers that when he arrived in 1948, for a career that spanned three decades as a Burnley player, he was quickly left in no doubt about the strength of feeling for the game and their local club. "This is a football town. We have had 50,000 at Turf Moor and you wouldn't be allowed to get that many on nowadays. Support for the club was huge. Even Central League games could get thousands coming to watch the reserves. I remember one game where there was 18,000. That is a measure of what football means to Burnley and though there have been a few lean years recently, where the gates haven't been as good as everybody would like, I think winning promotion to Division One has seen the club turn the corner."

He added: "In the Fifties and into the Sixties we were a great side and I don't care what anybody else says. We didn't have too many stars, but had a real balance in the side. Jimmy McIlroy was a great player, but he wasn't miles ahead of anybody else. He had his bad times, the same as the rest of us. People remember him always playing well, but it wasn't always the case. The other lads were just as important to the team. We had a hell of a good side and one that was settled. I can't remember many times during a season where anybody came in for any length of time."

The maestro himself Jimmy McIlroy recalls: "It is incredible when I look back and think of the top British teams in the Fifties and early Sixties in this part of the world. We had some wonderful derby matches with, not only the two Manchester clubs, but Preston North End, Bolton Wanderers and Blackpool. The days when the small-town clubs could compete at the top can't come back while there is no maximum wage. In those days, no matter how rich the club was, everybody was offered the same terms so there was no point in moving. While I certainly wouldn't advocate a return to the maximum wage, it concerns me what the future holds for the modern game. For all the money pouring into the game through television, it doesn't seem to make the majority of clubs any richer. All it does is encourage transfer fees and wages to rise."

The game also does not have the same appeal it had in his days. He added: "Football was the main source of entertainment for the working man. Television hadn't really taken over. There was nothing else for a fellow who worked all week to do on a Saturday afternoon other than go to the pub or watch a football match. Photographs from this era show full houses with spectators packed in. I think the football itself had more of a manliness about it. There were hard men playing and some vicious tackles. It was a man's game. Today there is a lot of pretending to be hurt, pulling on shirts and holding. Modern football can be like a wrestling match at times."

He fears centre-forwards from his day would struggle to get to the ball nowadays with all the illegal holding and obstruction that goes on. Players like Nat Lofthouse at Bolton Wanderers and Stan Mortensen at Blackpool would stand on the edge of the penalty area and come rushing in as the corner-kick was taken. Now they would never get a clear run at the ball. With the amount of sly, professional fouling that goes on, he wonders how the game will evolve in the future.

The art of tackling has also been lost. Where once defenders were noted for their ability to time a tackle and dispossess a player, that has largely disappeared. Given the age-old question of how players like Tom Finney at Preston North End and Stanley Matthews at Blackpool and Stoke City would have coped in the modern era, he is unsure. They would have had the skills and could beat a player, but he doubts they could get past their opponents' arms or if otherwise obstructed in some way.

"There are other changes," he believes. "In my time the best teams dictated the pace of the game. Now football is played at a constant, frenetic pace. I watched the Brazilians recently and it was sad because this wasn't a Brazilian team of old. Their 'samba' rhythmic play was gone. Once they could start it, stop it, play walk football and sprint football. Now they play at one fast pace. If even the Brazilians have lost that gift there is little hope for anyone."

Many of the highly paid and over-hyped players of the modern game do not impress McIlroy. He believes Ryan Giggs has failed to fulfil the promise he showed as a teenager as a dribbler of the ball. His Manchester United colleague David Beckham also fails to match his star billing. "I think Beckham comes in for more criticism from players of my vintage than any other player. At a recent tribute dinner held for me at Burnley, a lot of the old players were there and few rated him. He is a beautiful passer of the ball and he has vision, but after that he is limited. He reminds me of one of these American football players who comes on to do one job, but that is all they do."

Many other players of his generation, from those enjoying a kickabout in local leagues to the ones who plied their trade in the top echelons of the game, will also be nodding in agreement when the Irishman talks about the lightness of the ball in today's game. It allows for greater control, longer shooting distances and goals scored from more acute angles than in his day. It is also easier on the cranium for those attempting to head it, as anyone who has connected with the old leather ball, particularly on a wet day, will have cause to remember.

McIlroy acknowledges that even though they produced one of the finest sides of the last century, Burnley still struggled to shake off their reputation as an unfashionable club. He has no doubt about how the club was viewed beyond the Burnley town boundary. He recalls correspondence with an agent who had many famous sportsmen on his books. This agent said there were many opportunities to make money from sport, and he would like to act on McIlroy's behalf – providing the player moved to a London club. However, by the end of the Fifties, with exciting young players coming through and some attractive football being played, Burnley were able to shake off their tag as a dour, defensive team.

He added: "Burnley have always been regarded as just one of many ordinary football teams who never merited the headlines associated with Manchester United, Spurs, Everton, Arsenal and other members of the soccer aristocracy. We used to reckon that in terms of publicity, one good match in London was equal to about twenty in our home town. It's a handicap that all small-town clubs face and it exists today as much as it did then.

"Yet at Turf Moor we were always blessed with a wonderful team spirit. When we played against the glamour clubs, we felt we were tackling something bigger than ourselves. I know it may sound like some sort of football inferiority complex, but that's how we felt. We also knew we were representing a town that was solidly behind us. The fans were, and still are, top class."

He believes that the winning of the League championship in the 1959-60 season owed much to the work done in the Fifties to develop the club. McIlroy highlights the youth development policy at the club. Burnley were among the first to develop this before the war and it was continued in the post-war years. Whether it was introduced through foresight or necessity, it proved a major boon to the side. Players like John Connelly, Ray Pointer, Adam Blacklaw, Brian Miller, John Angus and Jimmy Robson all came through the club's own development structure and into the first team. There was also a training facility at Gawthorpe that was ahead of its time. For the fans the Fifties also saw the improvement of the ground with a new stand and floodlighting.

Yet while the post-war era is fondly recalled by many, there were distinct disadvantages. Certainly there was no disappearing after the game in expensive sports cars with the paying public getting just a brief glimpse of their heroes. The maximum wage ensured there were no fortunes to be made for the stars of those days. McIlroy remembers that there was no long-term financial security through football and no fortunes to be made for the stars then. When their playing days were over, there was the need to fall back on another job.

Now 78, Ambrose Allanson remembers being taken to Turf Moor in the Twenties. It is the way with sport that the heroes we remember best are those from our childhood and Allanson's greatest player pre-dates Jimmy McIlroy. He recalls seeing the prolific centre-forward Tommy Lawton playing in his two seasons at Burnley before the war. Lawton scored sixteen goals in only 25 appearances for the Clarets before being transferred to Everton for the then huge sum of £6,500. His keenest memory of a match was an FA Cup-tie against Birmingham in 1935. The price of admission had been doubled to a shilling for the game and Allanson feared he would be unable to go until an uncle gave him the sixpence he needed. He ran to the Bee Hole End and was to see all five goals in the match scored there. Birmingham went two up before half-time and then he recalls seeing the determined look on the Burnley players' faces as they got stuck in to win the tie 3-2. Going to watch Burnley has been an important part of his life. He soon had his season ticket for the new campaign in the First Division.

Keen supporter Brian Hollinrake was taken to Turf Moor by his father from the age of eleven, which meant he saw the side through the late Fifties and into their pomp in the early Sixties. For his early enthusiasm he was then to suffer through the wilderness years, because once a Clarets fans always a Clarets fan, through thick and thin. His own children have inherited his love of the club and in the 2000-01 season, granddaughter Eleanor, aged three, was taken along to soak up the atmosphere. You can't start them too young at Turf Moor.

He recalls what made it so special in those early years: "As a child we lived in Morecambe, but my parents were from Burnley and like many had retired to the coast. There was a sizeable support for the Clarets in the town. When I first went, it was unbelievable. First the size of the crowds and the excitement. I think at that time, for most people life was grey. It was an industrial town with its smoke and chimneys and then on a Saturday suddenly the team emerged in claret shirts and it brought colour into everybody's lives. At that age it was the colour, the style and the number of people that held me in awe. I didn't know Burnley was a small town. To me it seemed huge. This was a time when we didn't go on holidays and a trip to the football was a great day out. We had our set routine; after arriving in Burnley we went straight to Jax Snax for a cup of tea and a bite to eat, then on to the ground nice and early to soak up the atmosphere and then, after the game, it was back to the café for tea and to listen to the football scores on the radio before catching the 6.05 bus back to Morecambe."

As a committed fan who has never lived in the town, Hollinrake has his own theory as to why the supporters are so dedicated, even during the years of adversity. "The town is in an isolated valley that is cold and damp and has high unemployment and a poor health record. People are very proud of the limited things they have got and in their heyday the one great success was the football team. There are not many who change allegiance. They just wait and hope for better days and hopefully they are now on the way. The supporters always considered Burnley a First Division or Premiership club, even when we were in the old Fourth Division. I remember a miserable day at Rochdale and one frustrated Burnley fan shouting in desperation: 'For God's sake, get us out of this awful division!' Hopefully, trips to Rochdale and such like are now a thing of the past."

Promotion and a Cup Final

WITH the resumption of League football in the 1946-47 season, Burnley supporters were hopeful of promotion and a return to the top flight after seventeen years in the Second Division. Their optimism was fuelled by the arrival as manager of Cliff Britton, a former Everton and England half-back, whose promise was to get the club back into the First Division within three years. In the event he needed only one – and there was an FA Cup Final to savour as well.

After losing the best years of their careers to the war, Burnley's leading players like Harry Potts, George Bray, Reg Attwell and the amateur Peter Kippax were anxious to make up for lost time and show their pedigree. This was a side that would not only win promotion from the Second Division, but the following season would finish third in the First Division. Their strength was to be defence and the legend of the 'Iron Curtain' defence was born

Due to a severe winter the 1946-47 season would, remarkably, extend into the first week of June. And with a third of it gone, Burnley were top of the table and were well in contention at New Year, but it was to be their performances in the FA Cup that caught the imagination of their supporters. Their first opponents could not have been much tougher, with First Division Aston

Villa journeying to Turf Moor on January 11. To their amaze-
ment, Villa found the side from the lower division fitter and more
imaginative in their play and the Midlanders slumped to a 5-1
defeat. It was a magnificent Burnley performance with Kippax
the architect, creating the first two goals against a bemused
defence. Ray Harrison, playing centre-forward for the injured
John Billingham, and Welsh international Billy Morris bagged
two apiece and Potts also got on the scoresheet. Keen supporter
Donald Speak was delighted to see the return of football and
remembers watching one of the Villa full-backs leaning against
a goal post, completely shattered after Kippax had run him silly.
The heavy pitch had proved no obstacle for the wiry frame of
Morris either, he recalls.

A fortnight later, fellow Second Division club Coventry City
were the visitors and frost ensured it was a hard pitch. The
Midlands side had spent the week at Cleveleys on the Fylde
coast for some special training. The Burnley players had
followed their normal routine, although there was time for a
few rounds of golf. Jackie Chew opened the scoring after 31
minutes, but in a hard contest the game was not made safe until
five minutes from the end when a shot by Potts ensured there
would be no chance of a replay.

Burnley were on the road on February 8 to play Luton Town,
also in the Second Division, and while the home side were lucky
to avoid a defeat as Burnley piled on the pressure, the Clarets
were content to bring them back to Turf Moor, where three days
later a Harrison hat-trick ensured a quarter-final draw away to
Middlesbrough.

George Bray enjoyed Cup-ties because in all the rounds except
leading up to the Final, the team went for special training at
Southport. "We had some good times and there was a great spirit
without a doubt. We used to look forward to a Cup-tie coming
up. We were supposed to be under lock and key, but if you liked
a pint you could get one so long as you knew what you were

doing and didn't get carried away. There were some great lads and some characters who got up to a few things, playing jokes and larking about. What a laugh we had. They were certainly the good days."

Middlesbrough, who that season would finish mid-table in the top flight, were bidding to reach the semi-finals of the Cup for the first time and, having enjoyed a certain amount of luck to get so far, their fans were confident this would be their year. More than 53,000 were packed into Ayresome Park and they saw Geoff Walker put 'Boro into the lead with a goal against the run of play. Morris and Bray both hit the crossbar before a Morris strike in the 80th minute ensured a replay.

Fans were queuing before noon to get on to the Turf for the replay, but with the pitch frozen the referee did not give the order for the game to go ahead until 1pm and the gates were open ten minutes later. As the kick-off approached, many fans were still not in the ground and there were fears of congestion. Still fresh in everyone's mind was the Burnden Park tragedy of a year earlier, when 33 fans died and more than 500 were injured when an estimated 85,000 people crammed into Bolton Wanderers ground to see an FA Cup-tie featuring Stoke City. The local Burnley police thus ordered the kick-off delayed. Word was passed to the crowd outside Turf Moor and it helped ease the congestion. Jack Cochrane was a season ticket holder and owned a builder's yard in the town. He had finished work early to get to the game and waited in the Wellington pub for news of whether the tie would go ahead. "It was packed outside the ground and then suddenly the shout went up that they were opening the gates. The police shouted down to the crowd to let them know what was happening. We knew the kick-off was delayed and everybody calmly waited to get on the ground."

Forty minutes late, the game eventually started and the fans were treated to a memorable and hard fought Cup-tie that went into extra-time. Defences were always on top and after ninety minutes there was no score. With players tiring, the deadlock was broken in the first minute of extra-time. Tommy Cummings pushed a free-kick by Kippax to Morris, who settled the tie for the home side. Cochrane remembers the conditions were treacherous underfoot, but the Burnley players coped better and the slight figure of Morris was in his element as the bigger players struggled to stay on their feet.

Lifetime Burnley supporter Harold Gee was certainly not the only schoolboy who played truant to watch the match. His headmaster at Nelson Grammar had issued a strict edict that anybody absent on the afternoon of the match without a bona fide excuse would be punished. The cloakrooms were locked after afternoon registration, but Gee's arms were small enough to reach everybody's coats and the youngsters ran to the railway station for the journey to Burnley. "When we stopped at Nelson, my father got on and I had been told I couldn't go to the game. I had to hide in the toilet until we got to Burnley. It was worth it to see the game." For the youngster, the later semi-final matches were memorable for all the wrong reasons. He was in hospital having a kidney removed. It meant he also missed the Final and a trip to Wembley.

Ewood Park, the home of Blackburn Rovers, was the venue for the semi-final against Liverpool – who would finish the season as League champions – and tickets were at a premium with a flourishing black market and touts reportedly demanding three guineas (£3 3s) for a half-crown (13p) ticket. Fans began arriving in Blackburn from 5am and one café alone sold 10,000 cups of tea. Many walked all the way from Burnley, fearing the public transport system would be overwhelmed. A Burnley fan wearing a two-feet high top hat with the words "Wembley via Ewood" emblazoned on it, summed up the mood of the Clarets fans.

With a 52,000 capacity crowd there was a minor scare when two crush barriers gave way, but there were no serious injuries and those hurt were treated by St John Ambulance volunteers. In a tense match, nerves seemed to get the better of the forwards and Chew was particularly culpable when he failed to convert a simple chance in the first half. Liverpool's best opportunity came fifteen minutes into extra-time when Albert Stubbins (Sir Paul McCartney's favourite footballer, incidentally) profited from a rare error by Arthur Woodruff, but defender Harold Mather was on hand to save the day. For the third time in successive rounds, there would be a replay.

This time Maine Road was the venue and it signalled a friendly all-Lancashire invasion of Manchester. With both sides giving nothing away, the 72,000 spectators must have been preparing for extra-time when the deadlock was finally broken. Bray almost beat Cyril Sidlow with a free-kick, but Burnley had at least won a corner. It was taken by Billingham, and Potts and a defender both jumped for it, but the ball fell to Morris whose pass found Harrison. The centre-forward controlled it with his chest, swung round and hit a shot that the goalkeeper had no hope of saving. With so little to choose between the sides, one goal always looked like being enough to book a Wembley place and so it proved. Liverpool's best chance came when, unseen by the referee, Jack Balmer palmed the ball to Stubbins, but Burnley's defenders reacted quickly to prevent the centre-forward shooting.

Bray recalls: "It was always going to be bad luck on whoever lost because both were good teams and there was little to choose between them. It was a good game that anybody could have won. It was particularly special for Burnley because nobody in their wildest dreams thought we would get so far in the Cup and we surprised them all. What we achieved was marvellous and the people of Burnley showed their appreciation. It lifted everybody's spirits in the place. They came out in their thousands to cheer us back and it was only the semi-final."

Ambrose Allanson was at the game and remembers: "There were 72,000 people packed into Maine Road and the atmosphere was electric. The emotion when Harrison hit the ball first time and it went into the net was unbelievable. It was a huge release. The place erupted. The game had been so close, just as it was at Ewood Park, and both sides had chances up to that point. The other marvellous thing was there was no trouble between the rival fans. Everybody just wanted to see a good game of football."

Cochrane had set off with a pint flask in his hip pocket and such was the crush within the ground that at no point could he get the flask out. He believes that on the day, Liverpool were the better team, but Harrison was outstanding for Burnley and the Liverpool defenders couldn't relax with him. The amateur Peter Kippax also had a good game and Cochrane rates him as one of the finest left wingers he has seen. When he had the ball at his feet, there was a buzz from the crowd. His personal income, though, meant he didn't need to earn a living from football and had a love of golf to rival his passion for football.

The team were cheered back to Burnley virtually from the outskirts of Manchester and the closer they got to home the bigger the crowds became. Returning supporters drove ahead of the team coach and cheered and waved bells and rattles as the players went by, then raced ahead to repeat the whole process in the next town. At the hotel where a meal was laid on for the team, there was a huge crowd and one fan described it as like the VE-Day celebrations all over again. Just reaching Wembley was regarded as a great achievement. Confidence was high that the FA Cup could be brought back to Burnley for the first time since 1914.

In the League, results were still going well and Burnley were well on course for one of the two promotion places. The arrival of lowly placed Bradford Park Avenue on April 19 should have been a simple two points, but it was not to be. In what was the worst possible preparation for the following week's Cup Final, the Clarets slumped to their first defeat in 21 games – an unbeaten run going back to Boxing Day. The fans could only hope that the reason for the slump in form was that players' minds were focusing on the big day out at Wembley. Burnley even managed to open the scoring after six minutes through Potts and the same player was to hit the post, but two Bradford goals gave them the win. It was the first time that Burnley had conceded two goals in a game since November 16.

As preparations for the Final got under way, Burnley opted to stick with their usual training programme rather than move to an out-of-town camp. Demand for the 12,000 tickets far outstripped supply and there were complaints from long-serving supporters about the ticket distribution and allegations of cronyism in who received them. A sizeable chunk had also fallen into the hands of touts, which further angered the fans. Calls for a fairer system of ticket allocation were widespread.

Matters came to a head on Friday April 18, when a long queue that had waited most of the day to purchase terrace tickets was charged by mill workers pouring out of work and anxious to get to the front. Some had started the long wait for their tickets at 5am and there were an estimated 15,000 outside the ground when the gates opened and the tickets went on sale. Until a group tried to push in, the twelve-deep and half-mile-long queue had been orderly and good natured. Suddenly police were unable to control the crowd and inside Turf Moor, four police officers helped club officials to close the gate and the words "No More Tickets – Sold Out" were chalked on it. It was heartbreaking for those who had waited patiently. Women and children had stood all day and then been joined by their husbands when they finished work. The face value for tickets was from three shillings (15p) to £2 2s (£2.20). Later people were being asked for £2 for a three-shilling ticket, such was the frenzy of support in the town.

Other dodges were being attempted to get the valuable tickets. It was discovered that the season ticket coupon number fifty from 1939-40 season was identical to the 1946-47 season and postal applications were received using the out-of-date coupon. Also, shareholders who were entitled to purchase a ticket were producing certificates for shares transferred to them, so gaining more tickets than they were entitled to. The scams came to light when officials discovered there were more applications from season tickets holders and shareholders than were on the club's register. An official statement said: "Those members of the public who resorted to these tricks have deprived other members of the public of tickets."

Allanson had got his ticket because he was a season ticket holder. But even so, it had not been easy. "The secretary at the club at that time was very officious. When the tickets were on sale, I had been working overtime because I'd just got married and needed the extra money. All season ticket holders had been promised a Wembley ticket, but when I went to the ground this official said to me, 'You think you run the football club as a season ticket holder,' and didn't let me have a ticket. Fortunately the president, Mr Grimshaw, overheard him and said, 'This fellow is paying your wages. Give him a ticket.' Unfortunately I had to miss out on the big day because I had just bought a house so somebody else got the ticket. I listened to the match on the radio and we all had tears in our eyes at the end. It was heartbreaking."

As a youngster, Speak and a friend went for a walk while their fathers were in the long queues for tickets. The boys discovered that the queue for stand tickets was smaller, although the ticket price was higher. They went back and told their respective fathers who switched queues so that when the chaos erupted they were already in the ground and watched it from the windows in the stand where they had already acquired their tickets. Whatever the outcome outside, the youngster would be going to Wembley.

Cochrane was to miss out because, on a matter of principle, he would not take the ticket offered. He had seen the newspaper reports promising a ticket for all season ticket holders and as he was a season ticket holder assumed he would get one, despite a thriving black market and huge sums being paid. When he presented his book, though, he was told that the Wembley tickets were sold out and was given nothing but excuses. However, he was told that he could get the sought-after tickets through friends at the local Masonic Lodge. "I thought the way the whole thing had been handled was wrong. The secretary at the time was an arrogant little man and I argued with him about it, but he was having none of it. People were getting tickets who rarely went to Turf Moor. I listened to the game on the radio and it was a terrible blow when Duffy scored, but Charlton were a fine team in those days."

The town itself was gripped by Cup fever for the club's first visit to Wembley. In the pubs and clubs the match was the conversation on everybody's lips. Have you got a ticket? How are you getting there? These were the most asked questions. No team since West Bromwich Albion in 1930-31 had won promotion from Division Two and the FA Cup in the same season but Burnley were hoping to emulate that feat. The spirit in the team was high and the side boasted few big-name stars. Their biggest signing was the captain and rock in the centre of defence, Allan Brown, who was bought from Huddersfield Town for £1,000 in 1946. It proved a bargain buy. The centre-half was the hard man in the side and while at Huddersfield continued with his police career. Although he stayed at Turf Moor for only three seasons, he was a key component in helping Burnley successfully make the transition from Second Division to First Division football. In October 1948 he was transferred to Notts County, where he ended his playing career. He would return to Turf Moor as manager in 1954.

On the day itself, opponents Charlton – who had lost the previous season's Cup Final to Derby, 4-1 after extra-time – travelled from the hotel in Brighton where they had taken the sea air and played some golf. Left-half Charlie Revell had a knee injury and was replaced by the former Arsenal amateur Bill Whittaker, who had never played in a FA Cup-tie. Burnley were at full strength. The day was a sunny seventy degrees and the northern fans had transformed the West End with their rosettes and rattles and cries of "Come On Burnley." Some of the 17,000 who had made the journey slept in the waiting room and on benches at Euston Station until it was time to make their way to Wembley. Also cheering the team on were five members of the victorious 1914 Cup Final team. They were David Taylor, Billy Watson, William Nesbit, Bert Freeman and Eddie Mosscrop. Watson had with him the good luck charm he was given before the 1914 game, which was played at the Crystal Palace.

For Bray it was the fulfilling of an ambition. "I always wanted to play in a Cup Final. We were a footballing family and my brother Jack played for Manchester City and England and he was in two Cup Finals. He lost one, but then was on the winning side. I only got the one chance, but it was still a great occasion. I enjoyed the whole build-up to the match. I could hardly take in what was happening. The game itself went in a blur. When you are playing, you just focus on the match and even afterwards people would ask me about things that happened and I didn't know. The one thing I do remember, though, was the goal by Duffy. Beforehand there wasn't much in the way of team talks. I knew who I had to mark and we were more or less told to play our own game. It was a hard game I remember that."

Speak was thirteen years old and had never been to London before. "It was all very exciting. We set off at 11pm on the Friday night on a Bracewell's coach that left from Colne. It took us eight hours to get there and I remember being wide awake as we drove though London in the early hours. A chap on the coach leaned out of the window, ringing a huge bell and shouting, 'Hot pies, hot pies,' which the locals probably didn't appreciate, but the football crowd did. We caught the Tube to Wembley and it was a brilliant atmosphere. We should have won the game and we missed umpteen chances. There was only one team in it, really, and we kept thinking we would get there."

With Burnley's defensive record, goals were always going to be in short supply for Charlton, but unfortunately for the Lancashire fans their forwards also struggled. It was a game Burnley should have won, but with ninety minutes gone there was no score and it was extra-time. It might not have been needed if fortune had favoured Potts, who struck a shot of such power that when it hit the crossbar, it rebounded beyond the penalty area with Charlton defenders left to stand and watch. It was the best of a host of scoring chances that the Clarets managed to squander. Morris missed a couple he would normally have converted with ease, and Harrison had a strong appeal for a penalty turned down when he was fouled in the box. Burnley paid the price for their profligacy when, with 22 minutes of extra-time gone, a right-foot shot on the volley by outside-left Chris Duffy proved a spectacular way to win the Cup. Even then, the Clarets made a desperate attempt to pull level with Brown, Attwell and Morris all having chances.

Peter Kippax had played, but later went down with a fever and a temperature of 103 degrees which probably accounted for his poor showing on the day. He missed the return to Burnley, having been ordered to bed by a doctor. It may have been an off day for the amateur international whose family's interests in cotton mills ensured he was financially secure, but Bray pays him the ultimate professional's compliment when he says: "He couldn't have played any better if he had been a professional. He was one of the best and a good lad who mixed with everybody. Although he came from a moneyed background, he didn't have any airs and graces. The only difference between him and us was that we got paid."

Bray said: "I am not one for putting a lot of things down to luck, but it does play a part and we were a bit unlucky that day. Going down in extra-time is not a nice way to lose the Cup, but that's how it goes. Everybody talks about the chances we had, but all teams get chances during a ninety-minute game. It would be a poor do if they didn't. I'm not going to say Charlton were lucky. It was a good game and was obviously close to go to extra-time. We edged games in the run up to the Final and this one just didn't go our way. Ever since, though, I have always felt sorry for the losing side when I've watched the Final on television. It is not very nice to go to Wembley and come away with a losers' medal. I know, I did it. It's obvious somebody has to lose, but it doesn't make it easier when it happens to you. When we got back, we got a good reception for a team that had lost. It as amazing the way we were greeted on our return."

Speak recalls: "After the game, myself and my friend were really disappointed. We sat on a wall and a Charlton supporter came across to us and put his arms round us and said, 'Never mind lads you were the best team.' It seemed a long journey home, but we didn't come back straight away because all the men had gone into the local pubs to drown their sorrows. We had to sit in the coach and wait for them."

Tommy Henderson had been on the fringes of the first team during the war years and was to make two League appearances, but for the Cup Final he was on National Service and in Germany, playing for an Army side that included Malcolm Allison, then a Charlton player and later to find fame as a manager. Knowing that Henderson was on the books at Burnley, Allison asked if he fancied a bet on the outcome. "I said I'd have a small wager and he suggested £1. Given we were only on £1 a week in the Army, that was a hell of a lot of money, but I was confident of winning. After our game, we heard they were playing extra-time at Wembley and went to listen to it at a social club. Duffy's goal meant I was not just upset, but out of pocket as well. I had to pawn my pay book at a club for the £1 and they forwarded it the following week once they'd collected the wages."

Although Burnley had lost, there was still an unforgettable turnout back at Burnley to welcome the team home as they toured the town in an open-top bus with Cliff Britton refusing entreaties from the players to join them, instead letting them take centre stage. Outside the Town Hall, a huge crowd estimated at 15,000 waved and cheered behind specially-erected barriers and cried out for captain Allan Brown to address them. A local military band played *Pack Up Your Troubles.* The Mayor, Alderman R. Bushby, thanked the crowd for their turnout and the way they had welcomed the team back in such a magnificent fashion. He said that at the start of the season, few could have expected such success and now everybody in the country was aware that Burnley had a football team.

There was a huge cheer as Brown appeared on the balcony and, as the *Northern Daily Telegraph* reported, he told the crowd: "Every one of you is a wholehearted supporter of Burnley Football Club and I need hardly say that I am very, very proud, not only to play for the club, but to belong to Burnley. Naturally, we are just a little disappointed that we can't please you more by bringing back the Cup, but we have the consolation at least of knowing that in future matches we have to play, we have your confidence behind us and your wholehearted support, and with that I am sure we will get promoted."

In the League, Burnley put memories of their Wembley defeat behind them and settled down to the task of securing one of the two promotion places. A 3-0 victory over Newport County was a welcome return to winning ways, but then followed two defeats, including a 1-0 reverse at Manchester City before 69,000. The Maine Road club would win the Second Division title and the competition was now on for the runners-up spot, with Burnley and Birmingham City in fierce competition. However, representatives from the Midlands club didn't need to stay more than five minutes when the Clarets visited Leicester City on May 24, with Billingham scoring twice in that time. Jack Hays headed home a Chew corner-kick to increase the lead after fourteen minutes. Leicester had spent the week before the game at Skegness to prepare, but the sea air clearly didn't suit them. A

City fightback in the second half came too late and Burnley had two goals from Morris disallowed – the first for offside and the second for an illegal challenge on the goalkeeper. Future England centre-forward Jack Lee scored for the home side, but the last word went to the Clarets with a second for Hays in a 4-1 win.

Burnley could have clinched promotion two days later when they played neighbours Bury at Turf Moor before an expectant crowd of over 40,000, but in a disappointing game they could only manage a draw. Billingham opened the scoring, but Burnley squandered chances to seal the game and the equaliser came from George Mutch, whose extra-time penalty had given Preston the FA Cup at Wembley in 1938. The party was not put on hold for long, though. The Clarets travelled to West Ham on 31 May and clinched promotion with a 5-0 victory that stunned the Londoners. It was a superb display to record the biggest win of the season. Burnley were three goals up by half-time and yet again their defence was unbreachable. In the season Burnley conceded only 29 League goals in 42 matches to set a new League record. Harold Gee was playing cricket at Turf Moor on the day and when news of the result came through, the celebrations started. "People were going berserk on the cricket field and others were just walking round with five fingers in the air shouting, 'We're up!' Burnley were back in Division One where they belonged."

There was one more League game to play, however, and on 7 June 1947, Millwall held newly-promoted Burnley to a 1-1 draw at The Den before a crowd of 15,684.The thoughts of Burnley football fans now turned towards lazy days on Blackpool beach, cricket at Old Trafford – and First Division football come August.

The Forties

T HE remainder of the Forties would see Burnley consolidate their position in the First Division. The promotion season was followed with their most successful in the higher level at that point when the side finished third in the League. The bulk of the team were the players who had contested the Cup Final, but as the Forties ended, players who would be the rock on which the team was built for the next decade or more were being recruited. And none was to prove more valuable than the Clarets' greatest player, Jimmy McIlroy, signed from Glentoran in 1950.

McIlroy recalls that when he arrived, the Cliff Britton legacy of a strong defence still survived. It added to Burnley's reputation as an unglamorous club but ensured that the side had been able to consolidate their First Division status. It would take nearly a decade for the Clarets to graft consummate flair on to gritty defence and create a team that captured the imagination of soccer fans far beyond the town. However, even at this time, few teams relished the trip to Turf Moor where the crowds were partisan and the tackles fierce.

For the fans, the post-war years were wonderful, just to have Burnley back in the top flight and back in their claret and blue shirts. Donald Speak remembers seeing the team in the war years when they wore white and black kit. They had done so in the

Thirties, but thanks to enthusiastic fans who donated their clothing coupons, the club returned to the claret and blue that the players wore in their successful period after World War One. He recalls that it was a measure of the grip that Burnley FC had on him that on a hospital visit to see his father, who had never properly recovered from injuries suffered in World War One on the Somme, all he could think of was the Clarets' fortunes in a match being played at Grimsby. He toyed with the idea of trying to make the journey from the army hospital in Leeds to the match. Although he wasn't with the team in body, he was certainly there in spirit. He never missed a home game if he could help it and, if the money had been there, he would have travelled to the away matches as well.

A stalwart of the side was Tommy Cummings, who arrived in October 1947 and was to replace Allan Brown. Cummings was another player recruited from the North East, having been born and raised at Castledown, near Sunderland. He was brought up in a football mad area and played for Hylton Colliery Juniors where he once appeared in six local cup finals in a week, such was the prowess of the junior side. As a youngster, Cummings also played cricket to good local league standard.

Spurs had shown an interest and invited him down for a trial. He also played as an amateur for Middlesbrough. But a deciding factor in his choice of Burnley was that, not only had the club just recently been promoted and been FA Cup Finalists, their manager Cliff Britton promised a job in the local colliery that would mean the young player avoided National Service and would learn a trade. He said: "My father was a miner and he said football was a short life and he wanted me to have a trade to fall back on. Middlesbrough couldn't find me a job but Cliff Britton said there would be no difficulty finding me work as a mining engineer. That satisfied my father and he signed there and then. I didn't know where Burnley was at that time, but we were aware of the club and knew they were very strong. They had already acquired a reputation for finding players in the North East. In fact there used to be a joke that when we played Newcastle, there were always a lot of spare seats on the coach home because of the number of players from the North East who stayed up for the weekend."

Cummings recalls: "I arrived by train in a place called Todmorden and I hadn't been on many train journeys before. I was like a little boy looking out of the window and taking everything in. There was somebody from the club to meet me and we caught the bus to Burnley where they had arranged digs for me. There was another lodger, a Pole who was working at the pit, but when the landlady proposed taking in a third, it would have been too cramped so I moved to lodgings near the ground."

There were no palatial mansions in well-to-do areas for footballers in those far off days. For the majority of players not within walking distance of the ground, it was transport by bus and a chance to meet the paying customers at close quarters. If a player had suffered a poor game, he was soon made aware of it on the way home.

As a centre-half Cummings did not have a long apprenticeship in the 'A' team and Reserves, playing just a dozen games. The departure of Brown meant an early vacancy in the first team that Cummings was quick to fill. He would play for the Clarets for fifteen seasons and make 479 League and Cup appearances. He was selected for the Football League in 1951 and won three England 'B' caps in 1953, but narrowly missed out on full international honours. He made his League début away to Manchester City in December 1948. He coped well in a 2-2 draw. "When I went out against Manchester City, I looked around and these players were the ones who had been at Wembley the previous year. Naturally, I learned a lot from those lads and I think my enthusiasm helped them. I knew I needed a good game and I had one. I was a bit quick in the tackle that day."

There was, he remembers, a tougher test back in his native

North East a few weeks later. "I had just started to get settled in the side when we travelled to St James's Park to play Newcastle United and I would be up against Jackie Milburn. I was the youngest centre-half in the League, but I was exceptionally fast, that was a big strength of mine. I needed to be at my best because Milburn was a big strong man and once he got into his stride he took some stopping. He was a very good player and a really nice person off the field. We earned a draw and I had come through that early test well and it helped my confidence."

He recalls an anecdote involving Milburn when both were on international duty for England. Both were reserves for England when they played Northern Ireland in Belfast and were sat on the bench. "People were complaining that they couldn't see the match because we were blocking their view and then stones started being thrown. I was hit on the head with one and with that, Jackie picked it up and was all for hurling it back at the crowd, but I managed to stop him. There would have been a riot if he had."

Earlier Cummings finally felt as though he had arrived at the pinnacle of the game when, as he made his way from the train to the ship at Liverpool for the journey to Northern Ireland, he heard his name being shouted. "I looked up and there was Stanley Matthews heading for the same match. I thought, crikey, Stanley Matthews shouting for me. This is a good start to my international career." Sadly it was not to be and the full cap was to elude him as England manager Walter Winterbottom kept faith with Billy Wright.

During this period, Cummings was still working at Bank Hall Colliery and training on a Tuesday and Thursday evenings, but he admits that the pit bosses used to allow him to leave early to train with the first team players. This was to continue for his first four years at Burnley and the result of hard, physical work coupled with football training meant he was not only the youngest centre-half in the League, but also one of the fittest. It is also a far cry from the game today. One can't imagine a Premiership footballer combining playing with working as a miner.

The 1947-48 season finished with Burnley in third place. They were only edged out of the runners-up spot by Manchester United on goal-average. The champions were Arsenal. The highlights were two 4-0 wins, against Stoke City and, more impressively, Sunderland. On the downside, the Gunners had managed to do the double over Burnley, edging a close match on the Turf 1-0, but then enjoying a more comprehensive 3-0 victory down at Highbury. It underlined their role as a bogey team for the Clarets. However, it was the League runners up, Manchester United, who were to inflict the heaviest defeat of the season and for once make a mockery of the famed Clarets defence. They put five goals past Burnley and in the mill town there was disbelief.

Lifelong supporter Harold Gee recalls: "I was taken to Maine Road where Burnley were playing Manchester United. They were using City's ground because Old Trafford had been badly damaged in the blitz. It was New Year's Day and it was Burnley who were on the receiving end of a blitz. United ended the season as runners-up and they put five past us on a mud heap that wasn't fit for football. As we were travelling home through Burnley and Nelson, the weavers were coming out of the mills and they kept asking us the score. They didn't believe us when we told them. Nobody puts five goals past Burnley they said – and not many did."

During the Forties, Tommy Henderson played only a handful of first-team games for Burnley, but he was in the reserve side during the war years and then when League football resumed. He remembers the players returning from the forces and many were still in uniform in the dressing-room. "I remember Joe Loughran was a Major in the Army and on one occasion he had all the others standing to attention in the dressing-room. Everybody was just glad to be playing football again and there was a great atmosphere. They never exactly threw money around at Burnley, but they were still good times. It was a very sociable crowd. Burnley were strict about no drinking so there wasn't trips to the pub, but we played golf and generally everybody got on well."

Henderson had played some first-team games during the war, making his début as a sixteen-year-old, but now the return of the players from war service restricted his appearances. It is a measure of the wages a professional footballer received that although Henderson could have gone elsewhere, he was financially better off on a part-time contract with Burnley, supplementing the pay from his day job, rather than moving from the town to play football full-time. He was twelfth man at the Wembley Final, but the calibre of the Clarets side meant competition for a first-team place was stiff. He remembers great players like Harry Potts, George Bray and Reg Attwell.

Wing-half Attwell had signed for Burnley in 1946, after guesting for the club during the war, and was a key figure in the post-war years. Although starting out with Midland League club Denaby United, he had been a West Ham United player but made only one first-team appearance before the outbreak of war. Britton was to sign him for a 'substantial fee' and with Brown and Bray he made up the 'Iron Curtain' defence that made Burnley so formidable in the Forties. His failure to turn up for a match against Arsenal in 1952 hastened his demise' and in October 1954 he moved to Bradford City, where he played for one season before retiring from football. In all, he made 269 appearances for Burnley in League and Cup.

Behind the 'Iron Curtain' were stalwarts Harold Mather and Arthur Woodruff at full-back and 'Mr Consistency' himself, the goalkeeper Jimmy Strong. Mather was a skilled footballer who took care of his man, even if the winger was the legendary Stanley Matthews. It was said before a match where he faced the wizard of dribble himself, he would intensify his sprint training and attempt to prevent Matthews from cutting in by showing him the touchline. Mather was born in Bolton, but the usually efficient Wanderers scouting system had a rare off day in his case and Burnley were able to sign him just before the war. He had a few wartime appearances for the Clarets, but became a regular when League football resumed and played his entire professional career with the club. He still made half a dozen appearances in the 1954-55 season when he was 34. In all he made 329 appearances for the club. Although as a full-back he had attacking inclinations, the Britton game plan did not allow for them and he successfully adopted a strong defensive role. With Woodruff, few could rival the Clarets' full-back pairing at this time.

Woodruff was a Yorkshireman who joined Burnley from Bradford City in 1936 as a centre-half. It was only at the end of the war that he moved to right-back, where he was an ever-present for nearly six seasons before giving way to Jock Aird. By then Woodruff was 38 and, like many of his generation, had lost some of his best years to the war. Quietly spoken and quietly effective, his talents brought him two appearances for the Football League. He ended his League career at Workington, but, like so many former Burnley players, he remained in the town once his playing days were over.

In goal was Jimmy Strong and he was a man that could be relied on. From the resumption of League football in 1946 until March 1951, he did not miss a single League or Cup match for Burnley. It represented 220 consecutive matches and is a club record. In the Thirties he had played for Hartlepool, Chesterfield, Portsmouth and Walsall, but appearances guesting for Burnley during the war ended his nomadic football life when the Clarets signed him full-time in 1946. It would be December 1952 before he eventually lost the green jersey to Des Thompson, and he then retired.

Football can be a cruel game, as Henderson discovered. At the top level you get few chances and if fate is against you, that can make the difference between a successful career and being shown the door. In the Forties 'man management' was not in vogue and the axe could be swift, brutal, uncompromising and sometimes unfair. Henderson was chosen to play against Stoke City in 1949 and a nudge from behind in the first half saw him crash into the railings. He suffered a broken hand. "I hadn't been nervous about making my League début because I had been around for a few years and knew everybody. Our outside-right, Jack Chew, was injured and that's how I got my chance. Medical treatment then was poor and I had to wait until we got back to Burnley to get my hand seen to. I had been hoping for a decent run in the side, but the injury kept me on the sidelines. A month or so later I was picked to play against Fulham, but I wasn't match fit after being out with the injury. I was off the pace and it was probably the worst game I've played in my life. That was my last chance in the first team."

One of his favourite memories is of a pre-season tour to Spain in 1948, in which the opponents included both Barcelona and Real Madrid, and the Clarets never lost a game. As well as a good team-building exercise, it gave the players a chance to soak up the sun and see at first hand the Continental players' skills. Henderson remembers against Barcelona, the Spanish players were juggling with the ball to show their deft control. It had been agreed that the first half would be played with the lighter ball which the foreigners were used to. The second half would be played with a heavy English leather ball. Having watched the Barcelona players in the warm-up, coach Billy Dougall decided on a plan of action to negate the Spaniards talent.

Henderson explained: "I was sent to get the ball out of the dressing-room and he pumped it up as hard as he could, so it was as hard as nails. You hurt your fingers on it, there was so much pressure. Then he told me to go and throw it in the bath. Before the start of the second half, he dried it off saying, 'Let's see them juggle this.' It was so heavy our goalkeeper, Jimmy Strong, could barely kick it out of the penalty area. When their players tried to head it, they were sent reeling. Eventually Barcelona decided they'd had enough. One of their players kicked the ball into the crowd and we never got it back."

Jack Cochrane recalls that the Burnley defence conceded very little in the Forties. Lots of games ended goalless or with a 1-0 win for the Clarets. Manager Britton's philosophy appeared to be to give them nowt and hope to snatch a goal at the other end. Despite goals being in short supply, watching the team in action was worth the money and he remembers the terraces were packed. Everybody in the town took a keen interest in the club.

Harold Gee had first been taken to watch Burnley during the war years and, like all the boys at his school, couldn't wait for the start of League football once peace returned. He used to go in a family group and stand on the Longside, which after half a dozen or so terraces was ashes with railway sleepers. One of his favourites was Billy Morris, who used to pull his sleeves over his hands when it was cold and Gee copied him when he played football for the school.

He remembers in the 1947-48 season, Blackpool were the visitors and boasted an all-star team that guaranteed a crowd of more than 50,000. With his school friends, he was in his place by 12.30pm, otherwise they would have had little chance of seeing any of the action. He recalls a ferocious challenge by Allan Brown on Stan Mortensen that saw the Blackpool centre-forward leave the field. Nowadays it may well have produced a red card. In the Forties it was all part of the game. The sense the youngster had that Burnley could compete with the best was brought home with a Burnley win, thanks to the only goal of the game scored by Harry Potts.

For a youngster following football there is always disappointment to be endured. After losing in the Cup Final the previous year, Gee and his school friends were hopeful the team would get back and avenge the defeat at the hands of Charlton. For that matter, so were the players. It is a mantra always recited by the losing team that they will return the following year and make right the wrong. For Burnley, though, it was not to be as they limped out of the Cup in the third round in an ignominious defeat at the hands of Third Division South side Swindon Town. "I can remember the gloom at that defeat, but we bounced back with our League performances. By all accounts we never got going and just didn't click against Swindon. Perhaps the pressure of getting back to Wembley took its toll. Also, the heavy defeat against Manchester United had only been two days earlier."

There was better news in the Cup the following year when in the third round Charlton were the opponents and there was the chance to gain sweet revenge for the Cup Final defeat. Gee was among the 37,000 on the terraces to see Burnley go through 2-1 after extra-time. He said: "It was a great moment after what happened at Wembley. Replays had to be played during the daytime because there were no floodlights and the authorities introduced extra-time in the first game that season because too many people were taking time off work to watch midweek afternoon replays. At this time I never missed any games at home, but with transport difficult far fewer people tended to go long distances for away games. It was expensive and there were no motorways."

The euphoria of beating Charlton was soon dissipated as, after a win against Rotherham United, the Clarets lost 4-2 away to Brentford in the fifth round. In the League, results were disappointing and one home win in the last eight games saw Burnley finish fifteenth. It was a portent for the next four seasons when mid-table mediocrity was to be the Clarets' lot. In the last season of the decade, in 1949-50, they improved to tenth place and opened the campaign with a rare win at Highbury, with Billy Morris scoring the only goal. In the FA Cup, the Gunners turned the tables by winning 2-0 at Highbury in the fifth round to end the Clarets' FA Cup dreams for another year. The fans' hope was that the new decade would see Burnley build on the foundations laid in the Forties.

A New Era Dawns

WITH the early Fifties came the gradual decline of the 1947 Cup Final team and the emergence of a new generation of players who would do more than just guarantee mid-table finishes for the Clarets. While the first two seasons of the new decade were more of the same, from 1952-53 season until 1964 the team would never be out of the top ten in the Football League – a remarkable achievement for a small town club. Yet even in these successful years, a good early start to the season was so often undermined by a poor run towards the season's close.

Even so, the performances were enough to raise the spirits of the town as Burnley frequently proved more than a match for opponents with, on paper at least, a far greater pedigree. The early Fifties also saw the cotton industry that was such a staple of the town's economy, in sharp decline. In June 1951 unemployment was just 0.2 per cent or 197 men. By the following year that had risen to 15.8 per cent and 15,205 were out of work. The bulk of these were in the cotton industry. The success of the football team gave pride to a town being badly affected by a drastically changing economic climate.

Yet, as Jimmy McIlroy points out, in the early Fifties, Burnley had the reputation, despite their best efforts to shed it, of being a run-of-the-mill football club. They seldom challenged for the League or Cup but were rarely in relegation trouble. "We were a middle-of-the-table outfit. This was quickly brought home to me when I was transferred from Glentoran in the spring of 1950. Burnley ended that season in tenth place with the figures of an average team: Played 42, Won 14, Drawn 14, Lost 14."

Three of the defeats were in the last three fixtures of the season as Burnley's inability to maintain form to the end of the campaign was again in evidence. The opening fixture of the season had confirmed Arsenal's jinx on the club when the Gunners visited Turf Moor and took the points with the only goal of the match. The biggest win was a 5-1 demolition of Charlton in a match played before one of the smallest crowds of the season with only 20,008 watching. In the FA Cup, the draw handed the Clarets a tough opening tie at Aston Villa and it was the Midlands side that prevailed 2-0.

The season also marked the début of another Burnley legend, Jimmy Adamson, who took over Reg Attwell's number-four shirt with the veteran eventually moving to the other wing-half position. Adamson had been signed in 1947 and, indeed, in the early days there was competition between himself and McIlroy with both vying for inside-forward places, and the club coaching staff keen to move one or other of them to right-half. McIlroy was adamant that he didn't want to move. Adamson had no objections and the rest is history as he became one of the outstanding exponents in the position and was deemed unlucky not to win a full England cap. In the event he formed a famous partnership with the Irishman and when he won the Footballer of the Year award in 1962, it was Jimmy McIlroy who was runner-up – a measure of the strength of the Burnley side. In all, Jimmy Adamson would play 486 games for the Clarets.

McIlroy quickly got his chance in first-team football with the sale of Harry Potts to Everton for a fee of around £20,000, and completed the transition from Irish League football to the First Division, via the Burnley Reserves, in less than a season. He was to be virtually unchallenged for his place until his shock departure. He also proved wrong a local critic he overheard while playing bowls in one of the town's parks shortly after arriving at Turf Moor. The old bowls player and football sage was of the opinion that McIlroy was not good enough and wouldn't make the grade. It is to be hoped he was better at playing bowls than he was at judging football talent.

Also breaking into the first team in the early years of the decade was Brian Pilkington, who would remain until 1960-61 and be an integral part of the championship-winning side. He was one of the first of the young players who replaced the Forties veterans. After signing from Leyland Motors in September 1952, Pilkington made his first appearance in place of the injured Billy Elliott. When Elliott was sold the following summer, Pilkington's wing place was secured. He was capped once for England, against Northern Ireland in 1954, and also represented the Football League. The goal for which Burnley fans best remember him is the one against Manchester City in the championship-deciding match in the 1959-60 season. In his Burnley career of 340 games, he would net 77 goals. He was sold to Bolton Wanderers, and then played for Bury and Barrow before retiring.

In the 1951-52 season, while Manchester United and Arsenal were battling it out for the title, with the former clinching the silverware on the last day of the season, Burnley were again into their mid-table routine. Yet one match and one goal from this campaign has entered the town's folklore as Burnley's greatest goal. A few fans may make the case for another strike from the Clarets' rich history, but all of the 33,719 fans who were packed into Turf Moor on January 19 for the game against Newcastle United are agreed it was a truly memorable goal. The great Newcastle centre-forward Jackie Milburn described it as the best he had seen in his career, which is no mean praise. Surprsingly, though, the scorer was a defender – centre-half Tommy Cummings.

In keeping with the style of play of the era, the centre-half's job was regarded as purely a defensive one and in his 434 League appearances for Burnley, Cummings was to score only three goals. But his effort on this snowy January day was to be a gem. The game was tied with fifteen minutes to go. The player himself recalls that it had been a good game, but then it nearly always was against Newcastle. Morris had opened the scoring for the Clarets when, from a Chew throw-in, he dribbled to the deadball line and shot from the narrowest of angles. Milburn's 100th post-war goal, from a speculative shot, brought the sides level. The stage was now set for Cummings to produce his bravura effort.

On the edge of his own penalty box, Cummings intercepted a pass intended for Milburn and began his run upfield. Evading five tackles and twice switching the ball from his left to right foot, the centre-half's progress was unstoppable and then on the edge of the Newcastle penalty box he unleashed a powerful shot off his weaker left foot that the Newcastle goalkeeper Ronnie Simpson could not get a hand to. A huge cheer rose from the terraces and caps were thrown in the air. It was a few minutes before the hubbub died down, the congratulations for Cummings had finished, and the match could continue. The *Daily Telegraph* report of the match said: "When everything else about this game is forgotten, there will be talk by those who saw it about that wonder goal. What a goal, the like of which Turf Moor fans have probably never seen before."

Cummings himself recalls: "Everything happened in a few seconds and I didn't really have time to think. I just kept heading up the field. I said afterwards that I had just been looking to pass, but there was nobody available. Really, though, there wasn't much time to do anything. When I hit the shot, it could have gone anywhere, but it just flew into the corner of the net. I certainly never scored another like it. It was out of this world."

Harold Gee remembers another match that had them talking in Burnley, and not for feats of goalscoring either. Burnley played near-neighbours and great rivals Preston North End on Christmas

Day 1951 and it produced a nasty confrontation between England and Burnley's Billy Elliott and Scottish international Willie Cunningham. "They were knocking hell out of each other for the whole game. At one point, Cunningham was carried off on a stretcher and received treatment off the pitch, but then he shrugged off the arm of the trainer and ran back on and straight to Elliott. The other players had to stop him having a go. He wouldn't leave the field and Tom Finney, the Preston captain, moved him to outside-right, as far away from Elliott as possible. That cooled things off, but there was expected to be a return encounter the following day when Burnley played North End at Deepdale. In the event, though, the match was called of because of fog."

Fifty years on, Cunningham still remembers the incident and it provokes a strong response. "Don't talk to me about Elliott. He was a dirty bugger who kicked anything that moved." Gee has some sympathy with the ex-North Ender. He recalls: "Elliott was a niggly player. I had friends who were drinking in a pub where Elliott was drinking on his own. They recognised him because they were Burnley fans. Elliott called them over and said, 'If you've anything to say, say it to my face. Now piss off.' They hadn't been calling him, but were just remarking that he was a Burnley player. Being sociable wasn't a strong point for Billy."

An England international winger with five caps to his name while at Burnley, Elliott was not to be at Turf Moor for long as he was surprisingly sold to Sunderland at the end of the 1952-53 season, after just two years at the club. He had scored 14 goals in 74 games for Burnley, and for Sunderland he had a good career, with 23 goals in 193 appearances. He was replaced at Turf Moor by Brian Pilkington.

Sir Tom Finney remembers the incident and that such bad blood was unusual in the Lancashire derbies in those days. Although they were hard games, tempers rarely flared to such an extent. He recalls: "There had been a few things going on between the two during the game and I remember it finally came to a head when Elliott took a throw-in and as the ball was played back to him, Willie Cunningham went into him and carted player and ball over the line. The referee was going to send Willie off and I was saying things to him like, 'You can't send him off on Christmas Day,' and he relented after I promised to switch Willie to the other side of the field. It was an uncharacteristic situation and Willie was usually level-headed, but there had been a few things going on and he lost his rag. What more usually happened was we had some cracking games with Burnley over the Christmas period."

Indeed, it is a measure of the camaraderie between the players in the East Lancashire clubs that after his retirement in 1960, the great Tom Finney used to turn out in charity matches as a guest of the Ex-Clarets team. He has happy memories of the games saying: "Burnley were one of the first clubs to have an ex-players side and they played games and raised a lot of money for good causes. They were well supported and because I knew all the Burnley players, I was happy to turn out as a guest. It was a few years later before my own club Preston North End established a similar team. We might have all been retired, but there was still a lot of people who turned out to see us."

Tommy Henderson was an enthusiastic player for the Ex-Clarets side and remembers Tom Finney playing in a tournament in the Isle of Man. He said: "By this time, his wife was trying to get him to cut down on matches, but he had two pairs of boots, one of which he kept at work so that he could slip away for games without being caught. When he played for us, it was his third game that week and he has supposed to have retired. He was still very competitive. At half-time I remember him telling us where we were going wrong."

Charity games in the Sixties were to come later. Donald Speak has memories of the great football and great spirit in the game in the Fifties. He recalls the game against Stoke City shortly after the death of King George VI, on February 6, 1952, and the minute's silence that was dutifully respected by all. Then there was a friend who would be so inconsolable if Burnley had lost, he would take to his bed on Saturday night and not resurface until Monday morning, when he set off for work. Speak enjoyed trips to Blackpool to watch the derby game and then have a night out in the seaside resort before catching the train home. As he talked with the old fans on the long train journeys to away matches and listened to their tales of great players from the Clarets' past, one name kept cropping up as a rival to Jimmy McIlroy as Burnley's greatest star. The player they talked of in revered terms was Bob Kelly, who plied his trade for Burnley just before World War One and then up to the 1925-26 season. He made one short of 300 appearances for Burnley. For the old timers, Kelly was the inside-forward who had no equal. He had played for both the Football League and as a full England international and when he was transferred to Sunderland, for £6,500 in 1925, it was said that Turf Moor would never see his like again.

The animosity between Burnley and their neighbours, Blackburn Rovers, is well known and Harold Gee certainly subscribes to it. He tells one tale about how he believes the Rovers would go out of their way to inconvenience Burnley supporters if they possibly could. The Blackburn fans might have a different view, of course. In March 1952, Burnley were due to play Arsenal at Turf Moor in one of the highlights of the season. However, the following week the Clarets faced Blackburn at Ewood Park in the sixth round of the Cup.

Gee recalls: "We had been sent a small number of tickets by Blackburn, but we learnt that if we went on the day of the Arsenal match to watch Rovers Reserves, we could get a ticket for the FA Cup-tie inside the ground. A crowd of us went, got into Ewood, bought our tickets for the Cup, but the last thing we were going to do was watch Rovers Reserves. We took some sacking and put it on the broken glass in the window of the toilets, climbed out of the stand, waded across the river and got a taxi to get us back on the Turf to watch Arsenal. Unfortunately, not only did we lose to Arsenal, we got turned over by Blackburn 3-1. They just steamrollered us."

The 1952-53 season saw Burnley start well, and early in the campaign they were top of the table having won five of their opening six games. The next half dozen games saw them fail to secure a win, but they again rallied and were in with a chance of the title until a disappointing final run-in saw them finish in sixth place. Arsenal won the title and also inflicted a home defeat on the Clarets in the Cup. Gee remembers making his way by train to Burnley to queue for the tickets for the fifth-round Cup-tie. He stood for three hours before he had the coveted ticket. The queue seemed to stretch for miles and he remembers it being silhouetted against the skyline as he made his way to the ground. He hoped the match would be worth the wait, but Burnley were to be comprehensively beaten 2-0 on the day.

When Burnley fans of a certain age gather to reminisce about great games they have witnessed at Turf Moor down the years, it is never too long before an FA Cup match in January 1954 crops up in conversation. The visitors were Manchester United, the score was 5-3 to the Clarets, and four goals were scored in the first five minutes. Late arrivals asking the score could only look in disbelief when they were told. Burnley were underdogs for the third-round tie but were about to rip up the form book in the most comprehensive way possible. When Les Shannon was left unmarked in the United penalty box, he beat goalkeeper Ray Wood with a well placed shot. Then Bill Holden hit a speculative effort that might have been a cross or a shot, but either way it ended up in the net. It did not take United long to get back on level terms. Dennis Viollet converted a Tommy Taylor cross and then Jock Aird put through his own net.

Burnley fans might have feared that after their initial surprise in conceding two goals, United would have regained their composure and gone on to win. Yet with the pace of the game never letting up, it was the home side who got the breakthrough when a Shannon corner-kick went into the net via a United defender. Again United pulled level thanks to the skills of Taylor. The visitors were having the better of the contest, but against the run of play McIlroy shot home after a penalty box scramble. With 72 minutes played, Billy Gray scored Burnley's fifth, although given what had gone before, nobody was predicting victory until the whistle blew.

For Cummings it is a match that features prominently in the memory as he recalls his long career. "A lot of people hadn't even got into the ground and four goals were scored. As they are today, Manchester United were one of the top sides and their visits to Turf Moor always guaranteed a big crowd and a good atmosphere. How the events unfolded that day was just fantastic. The Manchester United lads came to meet us afterwards and we couldn't believe it. I knew many of them well from England trips."

Speak remembers the crush at the match as a mass of fans surged into the ground about ten minutes before the kick-off. "I was courting my future wife and we were on the popular side. There was a terrible crush against the barriers. I had a mark across my chest for weeks after. It frightened me to death and I've never been stuck against the barrier since. When the game started, though, I forgot about the crush. I couldn't believe what was happening, the way the goals were going in. United had won the League the year before and this was the first of the Busby Babes sides and neither us nor the United fans could believe it as events unfolded. It was a great game and a terrific day out."

Ambrose Allanson recalls that Burnley, in these times, were on a par with clubs like Manchester United and had a burning desire to cement their place amongst the elite. That season they finished seventh in the table and went out in the fourth round of the FA Cup, but only after an epic struggle with Newcastle United that went to a replay. While the training facilities at Gawthorpe were providing a conveyor belt for talented youngsters to come through to the first team, and the scouting system was operating efficiently, particularly with Jack Hickson in the North East, the Clarets were also not afraid to enter the transfer market. He remembers the excitement through the Forties and Fifties as the local newspapers told of another arrival.

He believes the loss of Hickson in the mid-Sixties amidst some controversy was a major blow to the club. The veteran scout was later to discover Alan Shearer and had sent players like Tommy Cummings, Jimmy Adamson and Brian O'Neil to Burnley in his long career working for the club. Burnley may not have been challenging for too many trophies during the early Fifties, but Allanson remembers it was a wonderful time to be watching football. "I used to go to all the home matches and there were some wonderful games. There were big gates and virtually every team had some star players. While we never looked like winning the League, we still pulled off some good results on the Turf. No team enjoyed playing Burnley up here. We had the makings of a good side. I remember Tommy Cummings' goal against Newcastle, but there were plenty of others that ran it close as the best ever seen at Turf Moor."

Jimmy McIlroy

SEVEN days after the turn of the millennium, a greying figure, now 68 but still lean and fit and instantly recognisable to Burnley fans of a certain generation, stepped out on to the Turf Moor pitch to acknowledge the acclaim of a packed crowd. Many showing their unstinting appreciation would never have seen the figure playing in his prime in the claret and blue shirt. All were aware, though, that the man before them was the legendary Jimmy McIlroy and that he was the finest player ever to represent the club.

McIlroy was the playmaker, the architect, the creative genius in one of the best English club teams of the last century when, either side of the dawn of the Sixties, Burnley were a dominant force matched only by their greatest rivals of the time, Tottenham Hotspur. In all he played nearly 500 League games for Burnley, almost another 100 for Stoke City after his controversial transfer, and represented Northern Ireland 51 times, including gracing the World Cup stage in 1958.

Sir Tom Finney, of England and Preston North End, played against him at both club and international level, in some hard-fought encounters. He says of the Irishman: "He was an outstanding player and one of the greatest of that era. He was a very skilful player and a great passer of the ball. McIlroy always stood out in my mind as the outstanding player in a very good Burnley side. It is probably a controversial thing to say, but I often wonder what players like McIlroy would have achieved if there had been a Great Britain side rather than him playing for Northern Ireland, where he was never going to be in the top flight of international football. The same can be said today with England not being able to find a quality left-sided player and people like Ryan Giggs not available."

The debate about a British side, and who would have made the line-up down the years, is one to occupy many an hour over a pint or three. As for the player himself, McIlroy still lives in the town, as he has since arriving from Glentoran in 1950. For the opening of the new stand he was joined by most of the 1959-60 championship-winning side as they took a lap of honour and brought back memories of Burnley's greatest days. He admits: "I was overwhelmed with emotion. I think we all were. From the day I arrived, I was claret all through. My friend and international colleague Danny Blanchflower was once in Burnley for a game against Spurs on a dull, damp miserable November day, and looking out he asked: 'How the blazes do you live in a place like this?' At the time I didn't have a ready answer, but I knew that this town felt like home."

McIlroy recalls playing at Highbury and Stamford Bridge and seeing leading celebrities of the day in the stands. Once the cast from a West End show, which the players had seen the night before, were there watching. He thought to himself that it would be wonderful to play before such luminaries every week. But only if these famous old grounds could, by magic, be lifted up and transported to Burnley.

The links with Burnley began early for the youngster born in the village of Lambeg, just south of Belfast, who had honed the skills which would serve him so well later as a professional by playing with a tennis ball. When he turned out for Glentoran as an amateur in the last match of the season in 1949, the Lancashire club had him watched. However, a Burnley director was of the opinion that he was no better than the young players already on the books at Turf Moor and the club were not interested. It was to prove a costly mistake. At the time he could have been recruited for the £10 signing on fee. Instead, McIlroy signed for Glentoran as a part-time professional, as well as continuing to work as an apprentice bricklayer.

Almost a year later Burnley renewed their interest and manager Frank Hill saw him turn in a terrific performance for Glentoran. McIlroy remembers: "I went into Belfast that night to see a boxing tournament at the Ulster Hall and as I returned later in the evening, I was met by my sister Doreen on her bike, who said there were visitors from England to see me. I borrowed the bike and headed home. Glentoran had agreed the transfer for £8,000 and I finished up with £750, which was a fortune for an eighteen-year-old. Every Irish boy wants to join an English club and this was my dream realised. It was only later that I learnt that the club had agreed to accept £6,000 with the remaining £2,000 going to me. I was young and my father had no idea how to negotiate terms. To this day I never found out what happened to the £1,250. The money would have bought a nice semi-detached house in Burnley at that time."

The story of his arrival in Burnley, after being driven from the ferry as it docked from Belfast, has entered folklore in the town. "As we pulled up in front of the hotel where I was to be staying for a week, I looked down the cobbled street covered in straw, cardboard boxes, rotting fruit and other rubbish left from the previous day's outdoor market, and I wondered what sort of a place had I come to. Such misgivings did not last long and I soon felt at home in this little town."

He did not have to wait long for his chance in the first team when inside-left Harry Potts was transferred to Everton. Having paid £8,000 for his services, Burnley now wanted their money's worth. They were not to be disappointed as he was to prove a bargain buy. He began his League career against Sunderland on October 21, 1950, before his nineteenth birthday, in a 1-1 draw when he faced England international Willie Watson and admits there could be no more challenging baptism into First Division football than against a player of Willie's ability.

He recalls: "The night before the game I was a bundle of nerves and couldn't sleep, but once I got into the dressing-room before kick-off, I was relaxed. I can't remember much of the game, but the following week was my first home game against Aston Villa and I remember my major contribution was providing the pass for Bill Holden which was the second goal in a 2-0 win. In both these games I felt comfortable and that I was capable of holding my own at this level. I wasn't over-confident. I remember playing against Wilf Mannion, who was a little genius, in a game against Middlesbrough and realising that I still had a lot to learn to reach his standard."

In the early days there were changes in position and personnel. The retirement of Billy Morris in 1952 saw McIlroy switch to inside-right with Les Shannon taking the inside-left berth. His right-wing partner changed from Doug Newlands to John Connelly. However, the forward line with which he is best remembered is the one that helped lift the title in 1959-60. In an interview with Frank Keating in *The Guardian*, after the unveiling of the new stand in his honour, the Irishman describes the occasion of returning to Turf Moor and being reunited with that impressive array of talent that represented the pinnacle of the game at the beginning of the Sixties.

After the others had taken their bow, it was the turn of the legend himself. He said: "Finally, it was my turn, and now I was treading my old field again ...and I was bathed in the arc lights once more. Just about every square yard of the pitch brought back a distinct memory to me in vivid imagery and recall ...a shot from here, a tackle precisely there, a particular pass from this precise spot, a goal or two, or just a little shuffle I once made exactly here ...it was uncanny, so intense, an almost indescribable sort of ecstasy, I suppose. I looked around and suddenly there were the four lads from the forward line, us five together again, waving up to the throng, drinking in the applause, embracing each other, old men now, but old men transported back, magically, to be forty years younger."

He praises the talent of the former players whose deeds have been etched in Burnley history. The speed of the right winger John Connelly, who could also cut inside and score vital goals. Jimmy Robson, instinctive inside-left, right-place, right-time poacher supreme. It was Danny Blanchflower's view that if it hadn't been for Jimmy Greaves, Robson would have been a British household name. Outside Robson was Brian Pilkington, whose one cap for England, McIlroy believes, was an insult to a player of his class. What Pilkington lacked in size he made up for in heart. And he had the talent to take on every full-back and whip over cross after cross. Sometimes the Irishman was the recipient, but usually it was the number-nine, Ray Pointer, who the crowd dubbed the 'pocket blond bombshell'. McIlroy said: "Ray had courage, verve and a non-stop engine. He was all oomph and nous with it. I saw Alan Shearer play only once, at Blackburn in his full glory and pomp and he was good. As I came off the ground with the crowd all abuzz, I thought to myself, 'Given the chance, who would you have chosen to play alongside at their peak, R. Pointer or A. Shearer?' And do you know, I still can't decide. For sure, Ray was utterly exceptional for his size; and only three caps for England, another idiocy of those times."

He said there were times when the team transcended everything. Although Burnley were only two points above a marvellous Spurs side at the end of the championship season, it was on occasions when everything worked in harmony that they realised nobody could stop them being champions. "A sort of purity, an utter untouchable magnificence, possessed us and we blended into one, each truly on song as in a single melody."

And he added: "That's why when we were all together again I found myself fervently wishing I hadn't been a player myself in those days, but a fan, a fan who was passionate about good football. When you're part of it, you don't obviously see the whole panorama – and, honestly, for four or five years and about half a dozen times a season, our Burnley side clicked in unison, and when it clicked it must have been utterly breathtaking to watch. I can't tell you why exactly, but we found ourselves caught up in excitement and charm and elegance and flow. Everything pinpoint exact, and all of us rapier sharp and on the very top of our game. I know it's ridiculous, but I wish I could have been on the terrace actually watching us play."

For those who didn't see him grace the football field and who want a neutral verdict from a man with an impeccable football pedigree, then the late Sir Matt Busby, in a forward to McIlroy's book *Right Inside Soccer*, published in 1960, gives a then contemporary insight into the Irishman's talents. "It is difficult to appreciate fully the skill of Jimmy McIlroy. For years he has virtually done the 'donkey work' in a team which, until their great 1960 championship triumph, failed to win the top honours in the Cup or the League. Yet for all that, he could be compared favourably with the greatest scheming inside-forwards. Jimmy McIlroy has the ability to stamp his personality on every match in which he plays. When he is at his best, he takes command of the game ...Jimmy undoubtedly possesses something, which may be indefinable, but which is shared only by the all-time greats."

Others who regularly watched him from the terraces at Turf Moor, or who played alongside him on the hallowed pitch, share the view. Peter Marsden was just starting out on his Burnley supporting career as McIlroy's days at Turf Moor were coming to a close. He recalls: "He was brilliant. We had a good team, but he stood out. When he was transferred it was such a shock that my mum came to the school gates to tell me. The whole town couldn't believe it. A factory owned by chairman Bob Lord had graffiti sprayed on it that was there for years. Nothing obscene, but things like 'Bring Back Mac'. Everywhere it was the subject of conversation."

Fans who saw him tend to use a single word to describe him: 'brilliant.' When pressed, they remember his skill on the ball, his ability to dribble to the corner-flag and hold the ball up with defenders unable to take the ball away, his penalty kicks, which were never blasted, but placed with precision, and the way he could dominate a game despite the frequently illegal attentions of defenders.

Harold Gee has happy memories of watching McIlroy. He believes there was more scope for players with the talent of the Irishman to express himself. Perhaps because the game was played with five forwards. Or maybe the individual skills hadn't been coached out of players in the Fifties. His favourite recollection is of seeing McIlroy thread the ball through the legs of the well-known Spurs hard man Dave Mackay, not once but twice. Burnley, at that time, had around eight internationals. They were good players in their own right around McIlroy, but he still shone out as the best.

Looking back on his career, McIlroy recognises that the life of a professional footballer was a good one, even if it didn't bring the financial rewards which his successors enjoy. It certainly paid better than his previous occupation of laying bricks and it gave him the opportunity to travel and see the world at somebody else's expense, while enjoying the best hotels and travelling first class. While his name was frequently linked with other, more high profile, clubs, he revealed there had never been any approach either through official channels or illegally. The only transfer request he ever submitted was in his early days when, after playing for Northern Ireland, he was dropped by Burnley the following week. His gesture, in a fit of pique, was quickly rejected.

When he did move, it was not at his behest and came at a time in his career when he would have been happy to play out his days at his beloved Burnley. McIlroy has only recently ended the mystery of why chairman Bob Lord sold him to Stoke City nearly forty years ago and plunged the town into despair. He believes his friendship with Reg Cooke, a boardroom rival of Lord's, was the reason he went on the transfer list. Many cite the decision to get rid of the Irishman in February 1963, following an FA Cup defeat at Liverpool, as the start of the demise in the Clarets' fortunes.

He recalls: "It was the worst day of my football career. I can remember Harry Potts calling me into the office at quarter-to-ten to break the news and say he was putting me on the list. Immediately I knew it wasn't Harry's decision because he looked in pain. He looked more stunned than I did, so obviously he had been told by Bob Lord that I had to go. In fact, some time afterwards, I learned from a Burnley director that Lord had called a meeting at his factory on the Sunday morning and he said to Harry Potts, 'McIlroy has to go.'

And I gather that Harry said, 'I still need him,' and Lord is supposed to have said, 'Well, either he goes or you go.' I've told this to many people and I don't think anyone accepts it. At the time, the support I received from the fans was overwhelming. Even after the move to Stoke, I still lived in Burnley. When I see old photos of me in a Stoke shirt, it just doesn't seem right. It only feels right when I'm wearing the claret and blue shirt."

As a lifetime supporter, Donald Speak has his own blunt view: "It was the biggest cock-up of all time as far as Burnley were concerned. We had always sold players to survive, but we gave him away. It was only a few months earlier that Bob Lord had said the Bank of England couldn't buy McIlroy. They said his form had slipped, but that was nonsense. As far as I'm concerned, that was the beginning of the end for Burnley as a major player in football. I used to admire Bob Lord because I thought he did a lot for the club, but at the end of the day he sold them down the river. He said he was a good businessman and everything he did was good business, but how could it have been smart to get rid of a player and lose thousands of spectators overnight."

McIlroy enjoyed an Indian Summer at Stoke City, helping them win promotion from the Second Division in 1963. He moved to Oldham Athletic in March 1966 and it was here he was given his first taste of management. He returned to Stoke City as chief coach and then in November 1970 was manager of Bolton Wanderers for just eighteen days after a spell as coach at the club. The Wanderers suffered two defeats in his spell, but it was not the reason for his early departure. McIlroy wanted to blood young, new players in the side because he felt the older professionals were not producing the results. However, his hopes of giving youth its head were thwarted by the chairman, who didn't have the same faith in the youngsters that McIlroy had. At the time, the Irishman gave the official reason for his leaving as 'unwelcome interference in team selection'.

Despite having been the victim of journalists who took advantage of his honest, open nature in his playing career, he now threw in his lot with the fourth estate, joining the *Lancashire Evening Telegraph* and then the *Burnley Express* as a sports reporter where he worked for many years. Now retired, he is able to devote even more time to his keen passion for golf. He has noted a recent revival of interest in the Burnley side of the Sixties. He still gets requests for autographs and to sign photographs, perhaps more than he did forty years ago. His achievements have been recognised both inside and outside the town. He was named as one of the 100 Football Legends for a 'hall of fame' after a vote amongst sports journalists. While in Burnley, as well as the new stand named in his honour at Turf Moor, a working men's club in the town has named its new £500,000 lounge after him. "A while back a couple of guys stopped me and said, 'We've been drinking in your bar,' and at first I thought they had mistaken me for a publican before I realised what they meant." It has to be said that few in Burnley would mistake Jimmy McIlroy for a publican.

Always the Bridesmaids

I N THE second half of the decade, Burnley enjoyed good League positions and enjoyed successful Cup runs, but they were still unable to take that final step which would bring the glory their play deserved. There were also some good teams around. Wolverhampton Wanderers won the title in consecutive seasons between 1957 and 1959, and a great Tottenham Hotspur side was emerging. The players who had been bloodied in the early years of the decade were now coming into their prime for Burnley. Success was soon to come, but for now they were to be perennial bridesmaids.

The 1955-56 season saw the team finish seventh in the League after a promising start had promised much more. The previous campaign Burnley were fourth with seven games remaining, but another disappointing conclusion to the season saw the team slide down the table. However, in 1955-56 the Cup caught the imagination of the fans and it featured a mammoth tie against Chelsea that took five games to resolve and left the players mentally and physically drained. The fourth-round fixture still represents a record tie for the club with Turf Moor hosting the first game, Stamford Bridge the return and then with St Andrew's, Highbury and White Hart Lane all providing the venue until Chelsea finally emerged 2-0 winners.

Keen fan Brian Hollinrake remembers travelling to Turf Moor for the first of the fixtures. "We should have beaten them in the opening fixture and the fans were disappointed. Chelsea had won the League the season before and had a good side and it attracted a good crowd with more than 44,0000 there and it was a real squeeze. For much of the game, I struggled to get a view, but it was a great atmosphere. The thing with that Cup-tie was that it seemed to go on for ever and with every drawn game it became more and more the topic of conversation as interest intensified. Given the size of the attendances for the replay venues, I think even neutral fans in the cities where the game was played got caught up with it. In the end, losing was a bit of an anticlimax." Within a month, Burnley beat Chelsea 5-0 in the League.

This was at a time when Hollinrake started travelling regularly to matches and he recalls that Burnley then boasted one of the smallest forward lines in the game. What they lost in size, though, they more than made up for in skill. The goalscorer in that opening 1-1 game against Chelsea was Peter McKay, a centre-forward not in the big, bustling tradition of, say, a Nat Lofthouse, but a slightly-built figure who was a goal poacher supreme. He joined Burnley from Dundee United in May 1954, at the age of 29, and in the 1955-56 season he became the first player since George Beel in 1931 to score 25 goals in a season for the club. He was transferred to St Mirren in 1957 because he did not fit in with the tactical plans of new manager Allan Brown.

Brian Miller was that rare commodity at Turf Moor – a Burnley-born player who made the grade with the first team. He recalls the mid-Fifties as a time of transition, with young players like himself who had worked their way up through the 'A' and 'B' teams and then into the Reserves, breaking into the first team. They would form the basis of the championship-winning side. When he arrived to work in the offices in 1952, many of the 1946 team were still playing. Players like Strong, Mather, Aird and Morris were coming to the end of their careers, while coming through the ranks were the likes of Adam Blacklaw, Jimmy Robson, Ray Pointer, Alex Elder, John Angus and John Connelly. There was still considerable experience in the side with the likes of the two Jimmies, McIlroy and Adamson.

Miller got his first-team call up standing in for Les Shannon during the FA Cup marathon with Chelsea in 1956. He recalls that players and fans alike couldn't believe it when match after match ended in stalemate. Both teams had chances to win it and, after playing football for such a length of time, whoever lost could consider themselves unlucky. For a successful Cup run, a team needs the breaks and it was not to be for Burnley that year. This was also to be only a temporary taste of first-team football for Miller. It was to be the championship-winning season when he finally forced his way into the side on a permanent basis and he was to remain there until the 1966-67 season. He won a solitary England cap, against Austria in May 1961. When his playing career was ended by an injury sustained during a match at Villa Park, Miller had made 455 League and Cup appearances for the club and was to later serve on the coaching staff. He was manager twice, from 1979 to 1983 and then again from 1986 to 1989.

He remembers: "With the young players coming through, and the experienced hands, we had a good blend and we knew we were a good side. The mid-Fifties were a transitional period and we came through that as a stronger side. With a lot of us having played together in the Reserves, there was a strong bond between us and a good spirit. We were a team that worked for each other."

Indeed, the 1956-57 season saw four players who would be key members of the championship-winning season and beyond, make their first appearance in the Burnley team. Some would then suffer the fate of homegrown Burnley players, of being sacrificed on the altar of financial expediency. The four who took their bow were the winger John Connelly, full-back John Angus, goalkeeper Adam Blacklaw and Jimmy Robson, whose goal in the 1962 Wembley game was the 100th scored in FA Cup Finals.

Connelly joined Burnley in 1956, after playing for St Helens Town, and although he made his début the same season, it would be two years before he became a first-team regular. In Connelly's first full season as a first-choice right winger, in 1958-59, only Ray Pointer scored more goals. He won twenty caps for England in total. His skills did not go unnoticed and clubs with tempting offers soon saw Burnley cash in and, to the dismay of the home fans for whom he was a favourite, he was sold to Manchester United in April 1964. The Clarets considered buying him back two years later, when he was ready for a move from Old Trafford, but figures couldn't be agreed and he went to Blackburn Rovers. He ended his career at Bury before retiring in 1973.

Right-back John Angus played more than 430 games for Burnley spanning three decades and won a single England cap that many believe was scant reward for a man of his talent. Always cool under pressure, he served the Clarets from 1956 until 1972, gaining a championship winners' medal and playing in the 1962 Cup Final before seeing the club for whom he played all his professional career begin life in the Second Division.

When Burnley's England international goalkeeper Colin McDonald suffered the injury which ended his playing career, Adam Blacklaw stepped up and was to play nearly 400 games for Burnley. He had made his début in December 1956 as a 19-year-old, but it was in the championship-winning season that he became virtually an ever-present, missing only one game in four seasons. He won three caps for Scotland. In July 1967, he joined Blackburn Rovers after losing the goalkeeper's position to Harry Thomson.

Jimmy Robson became a Burnley player on his seventeenth birthday in 1956 and was soon in first-team action when he stood in for Jimmy McIlroy against Blackpool and impressed with a performance that included a goal in a 2-2 draw. He eventually won the duel with Albert Cheesebrough for the inside-left position. He scored 100 goals for the club in a 242-match career, including five in an 8-0 demolition of Nottingham Forest in November 1959. In 1960-61 he topped the club's goalscoring table with three hat-tricks in seven games among his 37-goal tally. He left for Blackpool in 1965 and also played for Barnsley and Bury before retiring in 1973.

While young players may have been coming through, the season saw one of Burnley's key players in danger of having to quit the game through injury. Tommy Cummings suffered a serious cruciate ligament injury to his right knee at the end of the 1955-56 season that effectively cost him two years of football. It is a testament to his character that he was able to fight back and regain his first-team place. He said: "In those days, a cruciate ligament injury like that finished your career. I was sidelined for two years and remember the routine of training and trying to get back, only for the knee to break down again. I got to the stage where my right leg was an inch longer than the left because of the muscle build up with all the training I was giving the injured leg. I was determined not to give up, although it was heartbreaking at times. I did come back and was there for the championship, which made it all worthwhile."

Chairman Bob Lord may not have seen eye-to-eye with the supporters all the time, but he did share the antipathy towards Blackburn Rovers that was rife on the terraces. A snub when he was refused entry to the boardroom at Ewood Park when Burnley were playing there had not helped. His poor view of the Clarets' bitterest rivals was confirmed over the matter of Burnley's new floodlights. In 1956, when the floodlights were unveiled, it was Rovers who were invited to play the inaugural game. The visitors share of the gate was £800. The following season, Blackburn had their own floodlights, but Lord waited in vain for the invite for Burnley to provide the opposition for the official opening. Such slights against Burnley were taken badly by the chairman. He was said to be seething.

Even if League performances are faltering, a good Cup run can lift the spirits of players and fans alike. However, twice in the late Fifties, Aston Villa were to prove the undoing of Burnley in what was ultimately a period of disappointment. In 1956-57, the Clarets had been clinical against lowly opposition. Third Division North side Chesterfield were comprehensively outplayed in a 7-0 victory on the Turf. The next round was an even simpler task. And a more emphatic scoreline against non-League opposition. New Brighton, once a League club but now in the Lancashire Combination and having just knocked out that season's Third Division North champions Derby County at the Baseball Ground, were dispatched 9-0. It equalled Burnley's highest score in the competition, with the club having previously beaten Crystal Palace by a similar score in 1909. The Clarets even missed a penalty. Doug Winton failed to convert the spot-kick, but Brian Pilkington, who had been fouled, had been keen to take it in a match where players could do their averages the world of good. Both Jimmy McIlroy and Ian Lawson scored hat-tricks.

With the sixth-round draw it was down to more serious business and the visit of Aston Villa, although McIlroy admits he now began to think that a Wembley trip was a possibility because the Clarets enjoyed a good record against Villa at Turf Moor and the draw had been good for Burnley up to that point, giving a belief that the football fates were with them. Those fates, though, were about to deliver a cruel twist. An early own-goal gave the Clarets the lead and, although the side were not at their best, they held it until, with the clock ticking down, Peter McParland on the far post headed the equaliser. Burnley were to rue early misses by Ian Lawson, who replaced the injured McKay.

For the replay, the Burnley players had to contend with atrocious conditions of mud and water. A vigorous and robust Villa side were already being criticised for their style of play and the conditions were ideal for the home side. The Midlanders, who went on to win the FA Cup Final against Manchester United, won 2-0, with goals from Johnny Dixon and McParland. For the

Burnley fans, Villa were now firmly established as a bogey side in the Cup.

It is a curious thing with football memories that sometimes the most bizarre things stick. Jack Cochrane had travelled to the Aston Villa replay on one of a host of railway specials being run from Burnley. Thousands made the journey and were to be disappointed. He recalls: "It wasn't much of a game and I remember little about it, but on the way back we were standing in the queue for the train when the guy I had travelled down with suddenly remembered he was supposed to get a leg of mutton. Not wanting to get an earful from his wife, he left me to watch his place in the queue while he dashed off to find a butcher's before returning with the meat. I can't recall the match, but I remember the bloke carrying a joint of meat all the way from Birmingham to Burnley."

The following season, Burnley limped out tamely in the fourth round, losing 3-2 at home to Second Division Bristol Rovers after having forced a replay. It is a match that evokes memories for Hollinrake. He faced detention at Morecambe Grammar School on the day of the game, probably for not submitting homework. It meant that he was left with the prospect of sitting silently in a classroom for an hour or so instead of travelling to Turf Moor for what was expected to be the routine slaughter of an also-ran outfit from the lower division – and with Jimmy McIlroy and Jimmy Adamson dominating as usual.

He said: "I explained the problem to my dad and his solution was simple. I was to tell the teacher I couldn't do detention as I had an engagement at Turf Moor! Some hope, I thought. At afternoon break I trudged along to the staffroom and explained my dilemma and to my surprise and relief I was reprieved. The detention was cancelled and replaced by my having to submit an essay reporting the game. I watched half the game from the back of the Cricket Field End. There were over 41,000 of us on the Turf that night and the cloth-capped hordes in front of me meant that

I could only see half the field at the far, Bee Hole End. Still, I saw a glorious drive from McIlroy rocket into the net. Much of the rest of the action is either lost in memory or lost in the half of the field obscured by the throng. I do remember vividly the total feeling of deflation at the final scoreline. As for the essay, the teacher thought it was excellent, praising it as 'explicit and containing clear and powerful examples of pathos and emotion'. But perhaps detention might have been preferable after such a defeat."

There was a major highlight for the young Hollinrake, though. There has always been great rivalry between the East Lancashire clubs and although Clarets fans single out Blackburn Rovers as their particular hate team, Blackpool in the Fifties were also high on the list. And for a schoolboy living in Blackpool's neighbouring Fylde coast resort town of Morecambe, such tribal allegiances were particularly acute. The town boasted a good few Blackpool fans as well as a core of Burnley supporters. A good win meant he could hold his head high in the school playground, while the Seasiders' supporters were on the receiving end of the taunts. So November 16 was a particularly memorable occasion and a rare chance to see an away game as he made the short journey to Blackpool. There, the Clarets triumphed 4-2 with two goals for Alan Shackleton and one apiece for Cheesebrough and Pilkington.

"Preston were bigger rivals for us, but it was always nice to get a good win over Blackpool. I remember the game because it was another where I struggled to see. I was opposite the main stand and almost at eye-level with the pitch. It was with pride, though, that the next day I pasted a newspaper report of the match into the scrapbook I kept. It was written by Frank Swift, who was three months later to die in the Munich air disaster."

In 1958-59 it was to be another full-bloodied encounter with Villa in the sixth round. With Villa having a poor season – at the end of it they would be relegated – the Burnley team and supporters made the journey full of confidence. A goalless draw seemed to make a place in the next round close to a formality.

The return at Turf Moor, though, was to confound those hopes. For Hollinrake, the evening match meant a late night because it would be gone midnight by the time he got back to Morecambe. He travelled in high hopes and was also keen to see one of the Villa players. Peter McParland was a Northern Ireland international alongside McIlroy and the pair were in the news because the country qualified for the 1958 World Cup. McParland was to prove the undoing of Burnley and ensure the young supporter made the long journey home disappointed.

Burnley started well and enjoyed all the pressure. Yet they could not convert that pressure into a goal, to the increasing dismay of the nearly 39,000 fans packed on the Turf. Yet Villa had shown little in the way of attacking promise and as the second half began, Burnley still looked odds-on favourites. Then McParland received the ball near the half-way line and set out on a diagonal run towards the opposite wing. He kept running with the ball, getting nearer and nearer to the goal. With defenders covering an expected pass that never came, McParland's run took him to within twenty yards of the goal and his shot ended the Clarets' Wembley dreams for another year. McParland added a second later, just to add to the misery.

Although Burnley conceded two goals, the match gave Hollinrake a chance to see one of his Burnley heroes in action. He says of goalkeeper Colin McDonald: "Many supporters nowadays forget what a top 'keeper he was. It was no wonder Burnley kept so many clean sheets because he was terrific. An injury finished his career, but nowadays there would probably have been the treatment available to help him back to first-team action. I'm sure he would have played many more times for England, but for his career having been ended so tragically."

Indeed, McDonald is considered by many to be the best player to pull on the goalkeeper's jersey for Burnley. He was born in Tottington, near Bury, and began his football career at junior level on the wing. However, he would stand in when the regular goalkeeper was absent. He quickly showed he was a natural between the posts and, after a trial, signed amateur forms for Burnley in 1948, turning professional on his seventeenth birthday. It was six years before he got his first-team chance, but he quickly took it. Once he was a regular in the Burnley team, it was the turn of the international selectors to take note and after an appearance for the Football League in 1957 he won a full cap against the USSR in Moscow in May 1958. He played in all England's matches in the 1958 World Cup and was voted the best goalkeeper in the tournament. His career ended the following season when he broke his leg while playing for the Football League against the League of Ireland in Dublin.

Although Burnley may not yet have converted their promise into silverware, there had been a sea-change in the way the team played and how they were perceived in the wider soccer world. McIlroy explained: "Not so many years earlier, Burnley were a dull, defensive side. We conceded few goals. And we did not score many. As the Fifties progressed, our style changed. In place of the stodgy, 'stopping' soccer so often associated with Burnley, we substituted attacking tactics which the supporters quickly began to appreciate."

The Managers

HARRY Potts was Burnley's most successful manager and although his championship team was developed and nurtured by his predecessor, Allan Brown, he went on to develop other fine teams which underlined his managerial skills and ensured the club remained a force throughout the Sixties. To Burnley fans, the fact that Potts was at the helm when the Football League title was won in Burnley's greatest post-war season of 1959-60 is enough to guarantee him folklore status in the town. As a man, the former Clarets player was well liked and respected by his players and considered a good-natured, pleasant individual. Perhaps only someone with his easy-going temperament could have successfully worked with an autocratic chairman like Bob Lord. On the field, of course, it was a different matter, as his passion for Burnley and the game often ran away with him.

How important a role the manager plays in a team's success or failure is always open to debate. Jimmy McIlroy, for one, is keen to play down the significance of the manager in any side's success. He has an important role, of course. But the Northern Ireland international believes: "You can only be a great manager with great players. There is a lot of nonsense talked about what managers are capable of doing and what they are not. One of the important things is being in the right place at the right time. A look through the history of managers throws up loads of examples of ones who have enjoyed tremendous success at one club and then failed to emulate it elsewhere, or even subsequently back at the club where their reputations were made. Managers get blamed for far too much when it goes wrong. They carry the can for failures they cannot be held responsible for. Yet they also get too much praise when a team is successful. They are fated to be little gods when triumphant and heinous villains when things go wrong."

Potts was appointed in January 1958, after rumours that other, better-known, figures would be handed the job proved unfounded. Ambrose Allanson recalls that there were rumours Bob Lord had deliberately leaked the names of the leading contenders to the press. They were all still under contract to their own clubs and the furore which the newspaper reports created meant they hastily withdrew. Lord denied any involvement with the leak, but the newspapers had effectively left the way clear for Potts to get the job. And he was the very man Lord wanted in the post.

After a successful playing career with Burnley, where he was widely regarded as the first product of the club's policy of finding and bringing on talented youngsters, Potts' playing career ended at Everton. During his four years as a regular in the Burnley first team since making his début in the first League campaign after the war in 1946-47, he enjoyed a successful time. It included a trip to Wembley as a member of the 1947 side beaten by Charlton in extra-time. The best years of his playing career had been lost to the war, but he would find greater glories as a manager. A coaching appointment at Wolverhampton Wanderers was his first step on the ladder, where he learnt much from their legendary manager Stan Cullis. A spell with Third Division South club Shrewsbury Town gave him the chance to cut his managerial teeth.

Although Harry Potts was to prove a tremendous player for Burnley, Donald Speak remembers seeing him play wartime football when elements of the crowd were not overly impressed with the young newcomer. He was at a game against Sheffield United in 1946 when Potts, playing at inside-forward, missed an easy chance from close range. A fan shouted, "Potts for Rags," a chorus taken up by the crowd. As Speak recalls, he was soon to quickly prove his early critics well wide of the mark.

When Potts returned to Turf Moor as manager, he took over from former coach Billy Dougall, who had been promoted into the job and then been forced to retire early through ill health. He was, in any case, generally regarded as a stop-gap appointment since Brown's departure. Burnley were lying too close to the relegation zone for comfort and had suffered the ignominy of being knocked out of the FA Cup by Bristol Rovers on the Turf. Potts, born in Hetton-le-Hole in the North East, returned to the region and made an impressive start to his career as manager that was to continue for the rest of the campaign as Burnley steadily climbed the table, finishing a creditable sixth.

Andy Lochhead, who was a key figure during the mid-Sixties as a striker for Burnley, remembers Potts as a 'terrific fellow' whose abilities he only truly appreciated after he had moved on and served under different managers at other clubs. "He wasn't a hard disciplinarian and had an easy-going attitude, but after being at other clubs I can appreciate how good he was. It doesn't surprise me that he is ranked up there with the top managers the game has produced. He had Burnley running as a family club and blended a team that worked for each other."

As a committeeman at Lowerhouse Cricket Club, where Bob Lord was a leading member, Jack Cochrane helped organise friendly games against Burnley FC, who boasted some useful cricketers among their ranks. It brought him into contact with Potts who he describes as 'one of the nicest men you could ever meet'. However, Potts was not keen on the players drinking and he recalls at one Sunday afternoon game the manager approached him to ask if the bar would be open. He was told it wasn't because it was a Sunday. Potts was relieved to hear it. However, after the match and a lunch, the not-abstemious Tommy Cummings whispered to Cochrane, "Where's the ale?" The reply directed Cummings and a gaggle of players to the back room where, unknown to Potts, there was crate upon crate of beer for their consumption. What the manager didn't know about wouldn't hurt him.

Such was the Burnley tradition of keeping appointments in-house that Potts' coaching team were the very people who had helped him when he started his playing career. Dougall and Ray Bennion were still in charge of the coaching and would be valuable aides in his early days as manager. Cummings well recalls the coaching ability of Dougall and Bennion from his own early days at Burnley, when he arrived as a raw teenager before being quickly blooded in the first team. "I learned a lot in a very short time off those two. They were good coaches at that time. They wouldn't pass the exams needed today, but to us they were great motivators."

A former player who had sixty League games for the Clarets after signing from Falkirk in 1926, Dougall had joined the club's coaching staff in 1929 and was to continue his coaching involvement until January 1958, although he remained after that as club physiotherapist. He was ahead of his day in many aspects of his coaching, including his ability to motivate players and his quest for perfection on the training pitch. Nothing but the best would suffice for the Scotsman and players were forced to repeat moves until they were perfect. For less than a season he was in the manager's chair, between July 1957 and January 1958, while the directors looked for a replacement for Allan Brown. It was not a job that Dougall enjoyed and, once Potts was appointed, he was happy to get back on the training field with the players.

Jimmy McIlroy is full of admiration and respect for Dougall and all he achieved. He describes him as the forgotten man when people consider the success Burnley achieved, but a man who played a tremendous part in bringing about those triumphs. Players from the 1947 Cup Final side onwards thought the world of Dougall and respected his abilities as a trainer and coach.

McIlroy adds, however, that he wasn't cut out to be a manager.

He said: "As a coach, he had ideas way ahead of his time. He was the finest coach I came across in the game. The part he played in developing young players was unbelievable. I thought the world of him. I listened to every word he said and tried to carry out all the advice he gave me. I'm sure every player who came across him felt the same way. In those days the word 'motivation' was never heard, but looking back, he was the greatest motivator I have ever known."

McIlroy gives an insight into how Dougall psyched players up. He explained that at Turf Moor there was a long corridor down to the dressing-room, and just off it was the boot room. Dougall would be working away on the boots and would call him in as he walked past. Without looking up, he would ask details about a recent match. "How many tackles did you win? How many shots at goal? How many times did you find the opposite winger with a pass?" By the time the inquisition had finished, the player would be fuming, but equally he would be determined to prove a point to the old critic the next time he ran out for a game. McIlroy believes that Dougall was a master of psychology long before it became part and parcel of the game.

He added that Dougall also had a tremendous knowledge of the game and taught him many subtle tricks. He taught him how to shield the ball and adds: "Looking at some present-day internationals trying to do the same thing makes me cringe. They would have benefited from Billy's help and advice. When Burnley were at their peak we had a party-piece we used, especially away from home, when we were drawing or a goal in front and wanted to kill the game. We could waste time just by holding the ball at the corner-flag and keep collecting corners, throw-ins and then, when defenders got frustrated, free-kicks from fouls. We could use up ten to fifteen minutes in the closing stages of a game just by doing that. That was a tactic Billy had developed and instilled in us."

McIlroy added: "He set such high standards. If you were practising crosses, they had to be inch-perfect before you got any word of praise – and if they weren't, then you had to keep trying until you got it right. Billy was also a trained physio and a good one at that. If you had a pulled muscle he would tell you how long it would be before he could get it right. He was usually spot on in his assessment, but if he was wrong and it went beyond the date he fixed, he would claim it was the player's fault for doing something he shouldn't. He was idolised by the players. His pet saying was, 'Always do the things the opposition don't want you to do,' and it wasn't bad advice."

Potts, meanwhile, was continuing the successful formula that Burnley had developed to help them compete with bigger clubs with far larger cheque books. Rarely have Burnley managers been able to enjoy the luxury of going out and buying big-name signings. The manager himself put the secret down to concentrating on two major priorities. One was for the club to develop its own staff. However much the nature of football may have changed between the years just after the war, when he was a player, and into the Sixties when he managed, he always insisted that the raw material was the same. Burnley's much-envied scouting system, particularly in the North East, ensured a steady supply of youngsters, many of whom went on to make the grade in the first team. The second reason was the innovative coaching that Burnley helped pioneer. At a time when fitness largely involved simple keep-fit routines, with perhaps a practice game at the end, the players at Turf Moor were being put through drills in passing, shooting, dribbling and tactics under Bennion and Dougall. Potts always gave these two the credit for being ahead of their time in coaching skills.

So while he had inherited a team on the brink of success, he was also astute enough to build on it. Players who would be key elements in the championship-winning side, and later were brought through the Reserves into the first team, included Jimmy Robson, Gordon Harris and Brian Miller, while new talent such as Alex Elder was discovered. Combined with already established leading players like McIlroy, Cummings, Jimmy Adamson and Ray Pointer, the scene was set for the glory days that were to follow in both domestic and European competition.

Before Potts' arrival, the Clarets had been performing well and many thought they were poised to achieve greater things. It proved to be the case. Not only did Burnley win the Football League championship in 1960, they came fourth, second and third in successive years afterwards. When key players who had helped achieve such success were gradually lost, Potts brought in new stars like Lochhead and Willie Irvine. After a slight hiccup by their standards – they finished sixth and tenth in the old First Division between 1963 and 1965 – the following year they were back in contention for the title and eventually finished third, which brought a passport to European competition.

Potts was as fanatical about Burnley as any fan. And unlike Bob Lord, who refused to recognise any supporters' association and took no money raised by them lest it was the prelude to supporters wanting a say in the running of the club, the manager worked hard to build a rapport with the paying public. His programme notes were as biased as the fans could ever hope for. He called the supporters the 'Burnley Roar' and said they were on a par with any of the famous football terraces of the time like the Stretford End or the Kop. On the field, his emotions could run away with him. Most famously in the European Cup-tie against Reims, in Paris, when after running on to the field he was escorted to the stand by gendarmes. He also shared Lord's contempt for any journalist who filed disparaging reports about the club. A popular anecdote recounts how, on returning to his office, he found a radio journalist making comments with which he disagreed and promptly grabbed the phone and went on air to put his view.

After twelve successful years, Potts was moved from the manager's job to a largely powerless role of general manager. A classic case of a seeming promotion hiding the brutal truth that he had been removed. He stayed for two years before taking on the manager's job at Blackpool. His spell there included an FA Cup giantkilling when the Second Division side defeated First Division Burnley in January 1976. With the glory years long gone, he returned to Burnley in 1977 and stayed for two years with a side then in the Second Division.

George Bray, who played alongside Potts and then worked under him as trainer at the club, said: "He was a great player and a real gentleman. He was not one of our quicker players, but he was wonderful on the ball and a great passer. He had a tremendous influence on the players around him and it was always obvious he was going to be a coach and a manager even then. That he went on to fulfil that prediction, and at Burnley, is now history. He is one man who you can truthfully say never had an enemy in the world."

McIlroy added: "He inherited a potentially great team and built on it. I always think of him as being one of the nicest fellows I knew in football. Indeed, he was almost too nice to be a manager. I can't remember him ever swearing or giving a player a real rollicking. He did criticise, but somehow I always felt he was forcing himself. He was more like one of the players, joining in all our practice five-a-side games. At the same time, we were all aware who was boss and that what he said had to be done."

Allan Brown carried his 'hard man' reputation from the playing field into the manager's chair. Yet although he had been a key part of the 'Iron Curtain' defence in his post-war playing days with Burnley, which included captaining the 1947 Cup Final side, as a manager he brought more than just the defensive inclinations from those days. He also had a vision of how the game should be played which went far beyond a negative approach. One if his favourite sayings was that 'good football must bring rewards'. He had the ability to give players confidence and a sense of being valued. The very inspirational qualities that had served Burnley when he was a player and captain would now do so again. His strength of character meant he was not a man for players to argue with, but also ensured he stood up to the directors. When those power brokers included Bob Lord, his tenure at Turf Moor was always likely to be brief.

McIlroy recalls: "He introduced a lot of training ideas that were the vogue at the time. He also had what he called 'wicked eyes' and he could frighten the life out of you with just a glare. He was a players' manager and I always felt he gave players a fair crack of the whip. He was a man who wanted his own way and so did Bob Lord, and it was inevitable the two would clash. On the day that it was announced he was going to Sunderland, he took me to one side and said: 'It's breaking my heart leaving you lads.' He had introduced so many youngsters to first-team football and he realised this was a team that was on the verge of great things. It was only afterwards we learned of his confrontations with Lord. His last words to me were: 'One day you'll realise why I left.'"

Matters had come to a head with a number of disputes. In one, Brown had spoken his mind at a board meeting and his view was not the same as Lord's, which prompted ill feeling. A tour abroad at the end of the 1956-57 season hastened the end. After playing games in France, Switzerland and Germany, the tour should have ended, but Brown was keen to test his players against the Spanish club Athletic Bilbao, then one of the leading sides in Europe. The directors on the tour were against the idea, but had been presented with a *fait accompli* after the manager had consulted his players and found they were enthusiastic about the idea. The match was played and Burnley achieved a tremendous result, winning 3-0. It was at Bilbao's impressive stadium that Lord uttered his famous remark that this was the kind of stadium he wanted for Burnley. However impressed he was by the superb facilities, though, he was less enamoured by the way he had been forced to travel there. Within two months Brown was gone.

He had been instrumental in leaving a legacy beyond the playing squad. It was Brown who had first seen a marvellous opportunity to develop a training ground on fields on the borders of Padiham and Burnley. The 79-acres up for sale by auction adjoining Gawthorpe Hall would prove to be a facility the envy of many League clubs during the Fifties. Lord also claimed a starring role in the creation of the training facility, saying he ignored a directive from the board aimed at limiting what he could bid to acquire the site. Dressing-rooms, training pitches and a gym were quickly created, with manager and players involved in the hard, manual labouring work.

Brown was the manager when local man Brian Miller was signed and the player remembers a lot of talented youngsters arriving at the same time. "Harry Potts enjoyed the success, but the man who started it all was Allan Brown. He was a very good coach, especially with the youngsters. He gave me my first chance. I thought he was a terrific man on the training field."

Brown prided himself on being straight with people and being willing to forget personal differences in the interests of the wider cause. He was reliable and a man who knew his own mind. With a magnetic personality he had the ability to win players to his corner and command their loyalty. He once claimed he never left a club without at least some of the players shedding a tear at his departure. That was probably certainly the case at Burnley.

He had taken on the manager's chair in August 1954 from Frank Hill, who was in the post for six years and whose role had largely been to consolidate the efforts of Cliff Britton. After the war, Britton had steered Burnley to promotion and reached an FA Cup Final as well as establishing a squad of players that could hold their own in the top flight. Hill's skill in building on the legacy he acquired from Britton was to see Burnley finishing in the top half of the table in each of his seasons in charge. Of course, he also signed McIlroy from Glentoran.

Hill had enjoyed an illustrious playing career, being capped for Scotland and playing in the marvellous Arsenal team of the Thirties, with whom he won three League championship medals. Later, he captained both Blackpool and Southampton. His move to the coaching and management side of the game came in the season just before the war when he joined Preston North End as coach and assistant trainer. After war service in the RAF he was player-manager of Crewe Alexandra before joining Burnley in September 1948. After his time at Turf Moor, he returned to Preston North End. After a coaching appointment abroad, he became manager of Notts County. His last position before he retired in 1965 was as manager of Charlton Athletic.

It was Cliff Britton who had masterminded Burnley's post-war revival, aided by a squad of players who had matured during the war years when no properly organised League football was played. He was a former Everton and England half-back who introduced new tactics, notably in defence where Burnley were to prove particularly parsimonious in conceding goals. On taking office, he had promised a three-year plan to regain First Division status. He was to need only one. Key players like Allan Brown, Reg Attwell, Jimmy Adamson and Tommy Cummings arrived while he was in office. His time at Turf Moor was to be all too brief when he couldn't reject an offer to manage his old club, Everton, and departed in September 1948. In their first season back among the elite, he had guided the Clarets to third place in the League.

George Bray is full of admiration for Britton's managerial skills. "Cliff Britton had a good football brain and Burnley were lucky to have got him. He built a team around defence and he laid down the tactics to the team. He knew from A to Z what his players could do and what they couldn't. He had Reg Attwell in an attacking role, while I had a more defending job to do. He knew what he was doing and that was why we achieved so much. They used to say he was a religious man and his religion was football. He was also fair to deal with. If you had anything to come pay wise or whatever, he always listened and would sort it out."

Tommy Henderson also remembers Britton. "He was very respected, but always remained aloof. It was always 'Mr Britton' in your dealings with him. He was very strict, but very fair. He had been a hell of a player and was a hell of a coach. He was certainly a good manager for Burnley."

It was while serving with the RAF in Singapore that Allanson saw a newspaper cutting giving details of a Burnley win over Middlesbrough by 8-1. What caught his eye more than the match report, though, was the news that Britton was to be the new manager at Burnley. He recalls: "Britton had been well known as a player and Burnley had never had someone of his calibre as manager. I thought the club would be going somewhere when I read we had signed him, and I was right."

Champions

I T WAS Burnley's finest hour and the eventual realisation of
the dreams of all involved at the club and their fanatical
supporters. After failing to head the table until the last
match of the season, Burnley won an epic encounter away to -
Manchester City to finally be crowned League champions. Until
March, there was still an interest in the FA Cup and hopes that
it might be a Double. The League, though, was more than
enough.

Yet for Jimmy McIlroy, the 1959-60 season confounded his
own deep-rooted belief that Burnley would not win the League
championship. He always recognised that consistency is the
paramount virtue in winning the League. Teams such as
Manchester United and Wolverhampton Wanderers traditionally
produced consistent results throughout a full season in the
Fifties. Burnley, by comparsion, often struggled to maintain their
form throughout a campaign.

McIlroy reveals that even as Burnley's greatest season
unfolded, he did not believe that the club would finally triumph.
He said: "As season followed season, we seemed well-placed to
win either the Cup or the League, only to miss both of our targets
due to vital lapses in a few matches, or, in the Cup, due to one
bad game. I had the feeling, at the midway stage in the 1959-60
season, that, for the umpteenth time, Burnley would be proved

one of the finest teams in the game and yet win nothing. Happily, I was wrong."

At the start of January, Burnley found themselves in the top three in the League and the bookmakers also had the Clarets as a short-priced bet for the Cup. The Double was certainly on, although the Irishman was not as confident as the men laying the odds. Part of the reason for his pessimism was that Burnley were to triumph despite their leading player carrying a serious injury for much of the second half of the season.

McIlroy was suffering from a deep-rooted groin strain that first occurred during a game on December 12, playing against Arsenal at Highbury. In an injury-blighted season, a muscle injury had seen him on the treatment table daily for nearly five weeks before that game. After Highbury it was back to the treatment room. With the vital Christmas programme approaching, Burnley had to manage without the key figure of Jimmy McIlroy. That they were able to do so is testimony to the depth of talent at the club.

For Boxing Day's match with Manchester United at Old Trafford, the Irishman was on the sidelines. His deputy, Ian Lawson, was a success, scoring the first goal in a 2-1 win. But McIlroy was recalled for the return game at Turf Moor on December 28. That match was only five minutes old when all concerned realised it was the wrong decision. United won 4-1, and there was criticism for playing McIlroy half-fit, although the player himself says the decision was his that day, just as it was in all the games when he pulled on his boots in the second-half of the season when he should have been resting.

He recalls: "They were depressing days. I had reached my peak as a professional footballer at the age of 27 and was ready for what should have been my best season. Instead, suffering the anxiety of constant injury, it developed into my most unhappy one, although the final outcome was, of course, a memorable one. I was, for most of Burnley's greatest season, a permanent resident in the Turf Moor physiotherapy room."

A dose of 'flu meant that he missed the third-round Cup-tie at Lincoln. Burnley drew 1-1 at Sincil Bank, and McIlroy was picked for the replay. He played a key role in the goals. Burnley were awarded a penalty-kick which the Irishman converted. The second goal was scored by Pilkington, heading in a free-kick which McIlroy floated over from near the right corner-flag. With Burnley still in the title chase as well as the Cup, he sought advice on his injury from an old friend, Tom Finney, who played just down the road at Preston North End. If the player was looking for a simple solution, he was to be disappointed. Finney's advice sunk McIlroy into a deeper pit of depression. The England forward warned him: "I had exactly the same trouble last season, and like you, I played when I was fifty per cent fit. That nearly put me out of football permanently, so eventually I did the only thing possible. I didn't kick a ball for fourteen weeks."

McIlroy continued to be used in key games, including the FA Cup matches. He returned for the fourth-round Cup-tie against Second Division Swansea Town at Vetch Field. It was an exciting match, but not a good one. The pitch was muddy, heavy and wet. No goals were scored and the game went to a replay. With McIlroy again an on-looker, Burnley triumphed 2-1 but had to withstand some fierce pressure from Swansea in the closing stages as they frantically tried for an equalising goal after Burnley had been on top for much of the game.

For the third time, Burnley were drawn away from home. This time Bradford City were the opponents. The playing conditions at Valley Parade were a great leveller. The ground was too muddy even to allow the Burnley players to walk out and test it before getting stripped. No Burnley player felt enthusiastic about the match, yet the team started well and victory looked assured. In the first twenty minutes, Burnley found openings in the Bradford defence with ease and were guilty of being complacent in their finishing. It might have been a costly mistake because after half an hour, the pitch had churned up so badly that good football was out of the question. With the half-time score 0-0, Burnley were still confident, but that was shaken when, midway through the second half, City outside-right Bobby Webb scored the opening goal. Burnley were forced to throw everything into attack, and conceded a second goal through Derek Stokes with a breakaway against the run of play.

With only ten minutes left and two goals down, Burnley were very nearly out of the Cup, so they committed everything to attack and it paid off. Connelly ran perfectly through the City defence to sidefoot the first goal. With seven minutes remaining, there were 21 players in the Bradford half of the field. With injury-time being played and Burnley's away support fearing all was lost, Pilkington was fouled on the edge of the penalty box and took the free-kick himself. The ball was headed towards the City goal and hit the crossbar. In the ensuing scramble, the ball was forced over the line by Connelly.

In the replay, also staged in bad conditions with a hard frost making the playing surface treacherous, the ball did at least roll, and Burnley enjoyed a comfortable 5-0 win although it was not a memorable match. The turning point was a forty-yard run by Pilkington on the treacherous icy surface before passing to Pointer, who scored with a wonderful shot. For Brian Hollinrake, though, the match is remembered for an incident involving Pointer. He recalls: "One side of the pitch under the stand didn't get the sun and it was treacherous underfoot. Pointer ran for a ball and slipped, hitting his head on a white stone wall. The crack could be heard where we stood and I can remember fans thinking that he must be dead or seriously injured, but he just got up and carried on. He was a brave player and very busy and energetic. He always chased a cause, even if it was lost. There were nearly 53,000 on the Turf that day and thousands more locked out. That was a measure of the excitement which the club were generating in the town."

Harold Gee was locked out for the only time in his years of

supporting Burnley. This was a game where the congestion was so bad that John Connelly was forced to abandon his car some way from the ground and run the rest of the way to be sure of getting there in time for kick-off. That he got a goal showed the pre-match exercise had not done too much harm. Gee had travelled with a group of four, and one had pushed his way to the front and got in, so the others couldn't return to Manchester, where they lived and worked. There was nothing for it but to go to a nearby pub and wait for the end of the game. That they had missed a five-goal thriller made the disappointment all the greater. Over the years, during this successful period in Burnley's history many fans must have suffered the same fate and can empathise with how Gee felt.

With another Cup hurdle successfully crossed, McIlroy remembers: "Having struggled through every round, we had reached the last eight for the third time in four seasons. Now, and only now, I started visualising a trip to Wembley. The draw could not have been better for Burnley, with a home tie against Blackburn Rovers. We had avoided a clash with Aston Villa, our bogey side, and with Wolves, the team nobody wanted to face. Blackburn Rovers, not particularly well placed in the First Division, had done nothing to suggest undue strength. My only problem was the muscle injury which had caused me to play at half-speed in all my games since December 12. By this time, however, I felt that, even on one leg, I was getting away with things so often, there was no reason why I should not continue to do so, at least for the Blackburn Rovers game. Subsequent events were to prove me wrong."

Cup-tie tension, plus the added nervous strain of a local derby, produced 45 minutes of indifferent football, with Rovers slightly the better team. It was, though, to be the prelude to a second-half scoring spree. It started when McIlroy spotted Pilkington, standing unmarked on the corner of the penalty area. A pass to him saw a half-drive, half-lob shot go over the clutching fingers of goalkeeper Harry Leyland. Goals for Pilkington and Connelly followed and the tie looked to have been wrapped up. But a dubious penalty decision, when a shot struck Alex Elder on the boot and the ball ricocheted up on to his arm, gave Rovers the lifeline they desperately needed with only eighteen minutes left and Bryan Douglas scored from the penalty spot. A speculative shot by Peter Dobing beat the unsighted Blacklaw, and Mike McGrath stabbed home the ball from a mêlée in the penalty box. Burnley fans could not believe the events that had unfolded. That it had been their bitterest foes who had conjured such a miraculous escape made it all the harder to bear.

Hollinrake has no doubt that the Clarets were robbed. "The referee gave the penalty out of sympathy. Elder was devastated. The ball had hit his hand. For seventy minutes there had only been one side in it, but then it was all Blackburn. It made it harder that Blackburn were the opposition because they have always been the real enemy for Burnley. The fans hated losing to them. What made it worse that day was that the Clarets were always the better side. Everybody at the time thought Rovers would slip from the First Division and we would never play them again. Little did anyone guess we weren't to play them for years because we sank further than they did. I still hear people on a Saturday asking the scores for other games and when it comes to Blackburn they just say, 'How are the bastards doing?' and everybody knows who they mean. It was the same in the Fifties."

The Cup nightmare for the Clarets continued in the replay and this time there was no real doubt as to the winners when Burnley turned in a performance well below par. McIlroy's injury now caught up with him and a stomach illness also took its toll on Robson. The match went into extra-time, but within a minute of the restart Dobing profited from a goalmouth scramble and minutes later, Ally McLeod made the game safe.

Burnley minds could now concentrate on the League,where they were battling with Wolves and Spurs for the title. It was to prove one of the most closely fought and exciting League campaigns ever, climaxing in a nail-biting finale at Maine Road. The Clarets' cause in overtaking Spurs had been given a huge fillip on March 1 when the London club were the visitors to Turf Moor. The two clubs often produced outstanding games and Spurs did their part in producing a great match. Often, with so much at stake, skill and creativity can be blunted, but not on this occasion. There was an early scare for the home supporters when McIlroy went off injured, but he returned after a few minutes and, although playing at reduced speed, would orchestrate the best of the Burnley attacks in the second half. At half-time, both sides had enjoyed chances, but there was no score. The deadline was broken in the 65th minute when Connelly and McIlroy played a one-two and the winger then beat a defender and his cross was met by Pointer's header. Spurs increased their efforts and came close to equalising, but a 70th-minute goal for Connelly secured the points. It had been a terrific game and an interested American spectator, William Cox, who was organising a US soccer tournament that the Clarets would take part in the following summer, described it as a wonderful performance and promised that the team would generate tremendous excitement when they played in New York.

However, if a victory over Spurs had been a boost, they were to fare worse against their other title rivals when, later in the month, the Clarets travelled to Wolves and were on the receiving end of a 6-1 drubbing. It was a day when the Midland side hit imperious form and scored four goals by half-time. Burnley had their chances, but didn't get the breaks. Yet the feeling in the Turf Moor dressing-room was that this was not the end of the club's title aspirations. It was argued that the side had played well all season, but Wolves were tough opponents, particularly on their own ground. That they were to finish runners-up underlined their pedigree. Given they also won the FA Cup – by beating a ten-man Blackburn side, incidentally – it showed how close they had been to a Double. This was also, Burnley reminded themselves, a Wolves team bidding to win the League title for the third season in succession. So the players decided it was just one of those days and instead of dwelling on the defeat, they set their minds to winning the remaining games.

Easter saw the end of Tottenham's hopes when they lost two home games over the holiday period, against Manchester City and Chelsea. It left Wolves as the main threat, but when Burnley's two rivals met at Molineux it produced the best possible result for the Lancashire side with Spurs taking the points. As the season closed, Burnley faced four of their last five games away, yet they lost only the first, at Leicester City. A draw with Blackpool then saw Burnley travel to Birmingham City, who were involved in a desperate relegation fight and would always be tough opposition. The tension told on the visiting players, and what luck was going went City's way as Burnley played the better football, but didn't get the run of the ball. Pointer had a goal disallowed for offside and an appeal for a penalty, when Trevor Meredith was up-ended, fell on deaf ears. News that their fellow relegation contenders, Leeds United, were losing served to encourage City to renewed efforts and also lifted the crowd. Then, with less than ten minutes remaining, Meredith crossed, Pointer got his pass away as the tackle arrived, and Pilkington scored the vital goal that secured both points.

With Wolves winning 5-1 at Chelsea as the season came to a close, Burnley could look forward to their only home game in the final five matches of the season. Mid-table Fulham were the visitors in what was to be a disappointing performance. McIlroy was injured and would be sorely missed. The visitors did little in attack, but nerves took their toll on the Clarets and they couldn't get the vital goal. In the Fulham goal, Tony Macedo pulled off a string of good saves and in the closing minutes, when he appeared to be finally beaten, the ball was cleared off the line.

For Burnley fans the word 'if' had been frequently used in

conversations as everybody worked out the complex permutations which each result brought to the title chase. Now the situation was simple and the scene was set for the showdown at Maine Road in a game which attracted a crowd of 65,981. Wolves were one point ahead with all their fixtures completed. A win and Burnley were champions. Anything else and the silverware would again reside in the Wolves trophy room. Wolverhampton directors were there to see the drama unfold, as was their manager Stan Cullis.

Keen fan Brian Lucas travelled as a child to the Maine Road match. "I remember I only saw the ball once – and that was the highlight of the match. The crowd was huge and the atmosphere was amazing. A school friend of mine had gone as well with his father and he was on his dad's shoulders, telling me what was happening. When we had clinched the championship, everybody was celebrating. On the journey back we kept racing ahead of the team coach and then stopping and cheering as it went past before we sped ahead of it again. Lots of people were lining the road and many of the Burnley fans had walked to Manchester and back for the game and they were cheering. Everybody was late getting back as the celebrations continued. I was probably too young to fully appreciate what was going on, but I certainly got caught up in all the excitement. I would have appreciated the moment a lot more now, but I think it's going to be a while before we have that party."

Ambrose Allanson was best man at a wedding on the Saturday before the deciding match, when Burnley played Fulham. "I remember saying to my pal, 'Why did you arrange it for the day of the match?' We were stood in the church and the priest told us, 'I'll soon get it over with – I'm going to the match myself,' but there was no way I could get away. We tried to telephone the club to see how things were going, but the telephone lines weren't as good in those days. Finally we got through and were told it was a draw. It was all down to the Manchester City game."

He added: "I set off for Manchester straight after work and the traffic was tremendous. I feared we would miss the kick-off and told the coach driver to stop so we could walk the rest of the way because it was going to be a lot quicker. We weren't too concerned about whether we found the coach again afterwards. I told the driver if Burnley won the championship, I'd happily walk home. I must have been one of the last to get in the ground before they shut the gates. Nobody else on the coach had managed to see the game and there had been a bit of a panic when the crowd realised the gates were being closed. The City fans thought they were going to murder us. We were 2-1 up, but City were getting after us and Denis Law came close at one stage. I remember McIlroy had the ball in the corner and the City supporters were complaining that it wasn't football, but I told them that their players should take the ball off him then. They were tense closing minutes, but then there was euphoria when the final whistle went."

He took his young son to see the open-top bus bringing the team back, and carried him on his shoulders. It was a day he thought he would never see dawn and one he is unlikely to see again. For the passionate supporters of Burnley, it was their greatest day. He remembers the feeling of pride everybody in the town had at the championship win.

Jack Cochrane had to attend an important cricket committee meeting at Lowerhouse Cricket Club, but a telephone line had been rigged up to a local house to provide a running commentary on the score. When news came that Burnley were champions, the cricket club decamped to a local pub to celebrate before walking up Rossendale Road to see the all-conquering heroes return. All around, people were coming out on to the street to celebrate.

Tommy Henderson was a regular spectator as well as playing for the ex-Clarets side, and he remembers the championship-winning season with pride. "There were some memorable games. We used to go, not thinking would we win, but how many will we win by. That was a superb side. They were brilliant. From where I used to live you could hear the crowd on match days. The whole town was on a high. Everything was claret and blue."

In Brian Miller's illustrious career it was the finest moment. "It was the most thrilling occasion. The homecoming was tremendous. We didn't get into Burnley until late and there were thousands outside the Town Hall. They are brilliant memories and it was all the more special for me because I was born in Burnley and a local lad. I had supported the club since I was a small boy and first went to watch them during the war and in the Forties when they had some great players."

While in previous seasons, injuries to key players would have seen Burnley struggle, now there was strength in depth. Brian Pilkington, in a interview for a Clarets supporters website, explained: "At that time we dominated. We were a good footballing side. Everybody worked hard and everybody knew what everybody else was doing and we had a good squad of about thirteen or fourteen who could come in and play to standard. People like Bobby Seith, Walter Joyce and Trevor Meredith in the squad gave us a nice blend. In the Manchester City match, Connelly was injured, McIlroy played with his leg strapped up and Meredith came in and was outstanding. We had a really good squad. We won the championship, but I think we should have achieved a lot more than we did."

It was already gone 11pm as the victorious party approached the town of Rawtenstall on its way back from Manchester, and already thousands were lining the road. As the procession proceeded towards Burnley, the cheers and applause grew louder. The team were met by the Mayor, Alderman Miss Edith Utley, who told the players of the honour and the pride they had brought to the town. For most in the party it would be around 4am before they finally got to their beds. The following day, the local council gave a celebration lunch and captain Jimmy Adamson received the championship trophy. Burnley had at last got their hands on some silverware.

Falling Between Four Stools

WHILE winning the Football League championship confirmed Burnley's status as one of the major powerhouses of English soccer, at this time the two subsequent seasons merely served to underline that lifting the silverware was not a fluke as the Clarets continued to be a force to be reckoned with. Indeed, it can be argued that this side should have won more. In 1960-61, Burnley reached two Cup semi-finals, both the FA Cup and the newly-inaugurated League Cup, and finished fourth in the table. There was also the excitement for the town of European Cup football. They might not have had any trophies to show for the season's campaign, but the supporters had bucketloads of excitement along the way. As Bob Lord himself described it, Burnley had tried for everything and fallen between four stools.

Jimmy McIlroy, for one, believes the great Burnley side of the early Sixties should have enjoyed more success. He said: "Certainly I think we should have achieved more. Perhaps if we had a bigger squad it would have made a difference. We were playing a lot of games and there were not a lot of experienced players in the Reserves who could be called up. By the last few games of the season I felt that the team was a bit jaded and had lost its sparkle. That happened in more than one season. We'd played so many games and it takes its toll."

No doubt to the delight of Bob Lord and his fellow directors, success had been achieved while a healthy balance remained in the coffers. Before the start of the season Burnley announced they had made a profit of more than £13,000 and had a credit balance of more than £57,000. Season ticket sales for the new campaign had raised a further £29,500. The club's policy of relying on the products from its youth development programme, and not dipping into the transfer market too deeply, had certainly contributed to this. The fans, of course, would have liked to have seen one or two big-name signings and Lord, and the board, came in for some abuse. Yet to single out Lord for criticism is a little unfair. The other small town clubs in East Lancashire were adopting similar policies in order to survive. Bolton Wanderers, for example, had won the FA Cup in 1958 with a team that manager Bill Ridding proudly boasted had cost only £110, which represented eleven £10 signing-on fees. There was an inherent danger in adopting such a philosophy as would later be proved to both Burnley and Bolton, and indeed the rest of the mill town teams of the Red Rose county.

Lord himself took pride in the fact that a team assembled so cheaply could acquit itself so well. He calculated that the Burnley side which topped English football in 1960 had been put together for approximately £9,000 and were successfully competing with teams with a collective price tag of £350,000 or more. To his mind, it vindicated the youth policy and the effectiveness of the Gawthorpe facilities, and the coaches and trainers who put the young players through their paces. He believed small town clubs could compete with the big city teams despite the maximum wage being lifted. He did, though, believe that this needed to be coupled with no freedom of contract or else the talent nurtured by small clubs would be effortlessly poached. It was a perceptive view and Lord himself would have taken no delight in being proved right as, during his lifetime, he saw the small town clubs become marginalised.

To say that Burnley did not win any more silverware after their League championship triumph is not, strictly speaking, true. There was the FA Charity Shield, which opened the season on August 13, 1960, with Cup winners Wolves providing the opposition. Goals by Miller and Connelly were enough to ensure a draw and the two clubs shared the shield with each taking possession for six months. The fans had enjoyed their day out – although in those days the traditional curtain-raiser to the season was not played at Wembley – and honours were even in this match staged at Turf Moor before 20,000 spectators. Now the real business of the League could begin.

A win on the Turf against Arsenal provided an ideal start to the campaign. However, three defeats in four matches, including Manchester City doing the double over their Lancashire neighbours, was a setback. It was not to last. This was a side that, when it hit form, could take apart some of the best sides in the First Division. An example of the power of the Clarets at their peak came in October, when in four games they scored an incredible twenty goals. After a 5-0 win against Fulham, the team made the short journey to near neighbours, and great rivals, Blackburn Rovers, and handed out a 4-1 caning. But it was Manchester United and Chelsea who were to be the prized scalps in a winning run that had the fans drooling. In an eight-goal thriller against United, the Clarets won 5-3, and there was eight again in the Chelsea game, though this time it was more comfortable with a 6-2 result.

When Burnley won, they often won very well indeed. Unfortunately, there were too many defeats, which undermined the good work. With Tottenham Hotspur in commanding form in 1960-61, the League championship gradually slipped away. Burnley finished a creditable fourth and did have the satisfaction of humbling the recently-crowned champions when they visited

Cliff Britton, the manager who spearheaded Burnley's revival in the immediate post-war years when they reached the FA Cup Final and won promotion to the top flight.

Burnley skipper Allan Brown meets Charlton's Don Welsh before the 1947 FA Cup Final. Brown later managed the Clarets.

Frank Hill took over from Britton in September 1948 and will always be remembered as the man who signed Jimmy McIlroy.

Down and out at Anfield. Louis Bimpson scores Liverpool's third in their 4-0 win over Burnley in September 1953. The Clarets' season is best remembered for a 5-3 FA Cup victory over Manchester United.

Burnley team pictured at Gawthorpe Hall in 1955. The goalkeeper is Colin McDonald who made 201 first-team appearances and won eight full caps, playing in all England's matches in the 1958 World Cup.

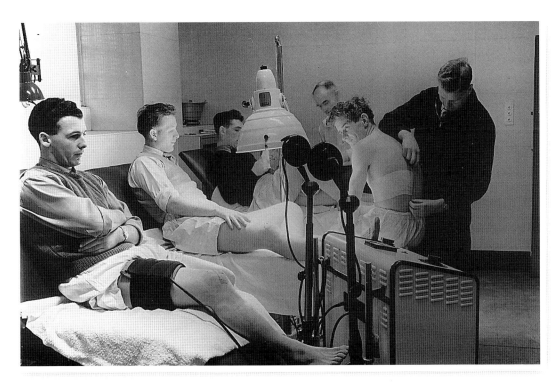

Busy treatment room at Turf Moor in January 1956.

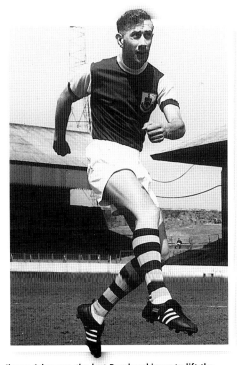

Jimmy Adamson, the last Burnley skipper to lift the League Championship trophy and to lead the Clarets out to an FA Cup Final. He made 486 senior appearances overall and later proved a successful manager at Turf Moor. Like Cummings, full international honours eluded him.

Tommy Cummings made 479 appearances for Burnley and scored three goals, one of them 'the greatest ever scored at Turf Moor'. His Burnley career lasted 15 years and was played out in three decades.

Colin McDonald watches a header from Blackburn's Ally McLeod go past the post at Turf Moor in October 1958. Jimmy Adamson and Bryan Douglas (Blackburn) also look on. The result was a goalless draw.

John Connelly and his workmates at Bank Hall Colliery after he had been called up for his first of ten England caps with Burnley, against Wales in October 1959. He made 265 senior appearances for Burnley, scoring 105 goals before being transferred to Manchester United.

Harry Potts, the former Burnley player who managed the club to the League title and an FA Cup Final. He also guided them into their first-ever season of European football.

Jimmy McIlroy, 'the greatest player ever to wear Burnley's colours'. McIlroy made 497 senior appearances and scored 131 goals before being controversially transferred in 1963. He inspired Burnley to the League title and into Europe and won 51 Northern Ireland caps while at Turf Moor, also playing for Great Britain against the Rest of Europe.

Brian Pilkington scored 77 goals in 340 games for Burnley between 1952-53 and 1960-61, missing only one game in the League championship-winning season. He won his one England cap in Belfast in October 1954.

Albert Cheesebrough, one of the few Burnley-born players to have appeared for the Clarets. He scored 40 goals in 158 League and Cup games from 1951-52 to 1959-60.

Adam Blacklaw kept goal for Burnley on 383 occasions, taking over from Colin McDonald when the England goalkeeper had to retire through injury. He won three caps for Scotland. Blacklaw missed only one game when Burnley won the League title in 1959-60 and in the next four seasons missed only one game.

Ray Pointer had a remarkable strike rate for Burnley – 133 goals in 270 League and Cup matches between 1957-58 and 1964-65. He won three full caps for England, played in the League championship-winning side and in the 1962 FA Cup Final. And all this after being rejected as a youngster by Blackpool!

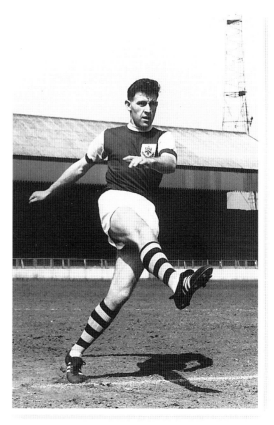

Alex Elder made 330 senior appearances for Burnley between 1959-60 and 1966-67, making his debut in the League Championship-winning season. He won 34 Northern Ireland caps while with the Clarets.

John Angus made a remarkable 521 senior appearances for Burnley, from 1956-57 to 1971-72. On his one appearance for England, manager Walter Winterbottom described it as the best international debut he had ever seen.

Alex Elder, John Connelly, Walter Joyce, John Angus, Brian Miller and Jimmy Robson training on Burnley cricket ground.

Jimmy McIlroy scores in the 5-3 victory over Manchester United at the Turf in October 1960.

Jimmy McIlroy sees his shot hit the post in the last minute of the European Cup quarter-final match against SV Hamburg at Turf Moor in January 1961.

Ian Towers scores in the 1-1 draw against Chelsea at the Turf in April 1962.

"We can lick anything…" Burnley players line up for a refreshing ice-cream apiece before the 1962 FA Cup Final against Tottenham Hotspur.

Skipper Jimmy Adamson has a taste of cheese from the English Cheese Maiden, watched by his Cup Final teammates.

The 1962 Cup Final team and reserves pictured on the eve of the Wembley game.

Jimmy Greaves (extreme left) watches his effort beat Adam Blacklaw for the first goal of the 1962 FA Cup Final.

Jimmy Adamson and Spurs skipper Danny Blanchflower greet each other at Wembley.

Bob Lord (right) with Field Marshal Montgomery and the Mayor of Burnley before the Burnley-Leeds game at Turf Moor in May 1966.

Andy Lochhead nips in front of Gordon Banks to score in the
4-0 win over Stoke City at the Turf in April 1968.

Frank Casper heads home in the 5-1 home win over Leeds
United in October 1968. Gary Sprake looks on helplessly.

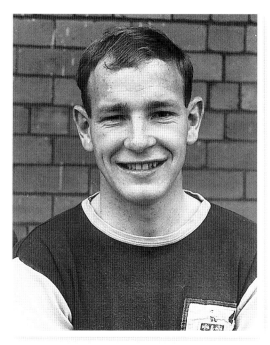

Andy Lochhead scored three goals in five games in his first season with Burnley's first team, in 1960-61 when he deputised for Ray Pointer. He finally established a regular place in 1962-63 and went on to hit 128 goals in 266 senior games for the Clarets including five goals in a match twice.

Ralph Coates joined Burnley as a 16-year-old and played in 261 senior games, scoring 32 goals, before joining Spurs in 1971, at a time when the Clarets were forced to sell their better players. A great favourite at the Turf, Coates was a full England international and a member of the 1970 World Cup finals squad.

Probably Burnley's greatest player of the post-McIlroy era, England international Martin Dobson made 499 first-team appearances for the Clarets, scoring 76 goals. These came in two spells at Turf Moor. In August 1974 he left for Everton for £300,000 and exactly five years later was re-signed from the Merseysiders for £100,000. Dobson captained two Burnley title-winning sides, in 1972-73 and 1981-82.

Frank Casper joined Burnley for £30,000 from Rotherham United in the 1967 close season, scored on his debut and was the Clarets' leading scorer in his first two seasons. He managed six games in Burnley's last season in the top flight, 1975-76, but his career had effectively ended in a Norman Hunter tackle at Elland Road two seasons earlier. Casper scored 89 goals in 275 games for Burnley.

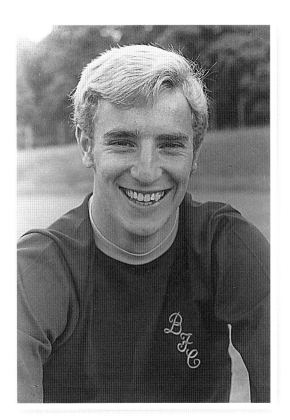

Colin Waldron made 356 appearances in Burnley's first team after signing from Chelsea in 1967. His signing, along with that of Frank Casper, came at a time when Burnley were famous for not buying players, and thus bucked a trend. Waldron scored 18 goals for Burnley, one of them in the dying moment of the 1972-73 season at Deepdale which earned the Clarets the Second Division championship.

Burnley team in November 1968. Back row (left to right): Blant, Dobson, Thomson, Waldron, Kindon, Collins. Front row: Latcham, Smith, Murray, Coates, Casper, Thomas.

on April 22, as the season drew to a close. It was a performance that put the soon-to-be Double winners in the shade. In the first half, Scottish international goalkeeper Bill Brown frustrated Burnley and after the visitors had been given a warm reception by the crowd, Spurs took a two-goal lead and, although the scoreline flattered them, it looked as though they would be celebrating their title achievement in fine style. In the second half, though, Burnley put on a display worthy of defending champions and this time Brown could not save the Londoners. There were two goals for Gordon Harris and one each for Jimmy Robson and Jimmy McIlroy.

Harris was famed for his powerful shooting with his left foot. He arrived at Turf Moor in 1958, after playing for a colliery team near his home town of Worksop in Nottinghamshire. Opportunities for first-team football were limited while Brian Pilkington remained, but Pilkington's departure to Bolton Wanderers allowed Harris to establish himself in the side. Not a man to be trifled with, there were the occasional bust-ups with colleagues on the training field and a few run-ins with referees. He had made 313 appearances by the time he was transferred to Sunderland for a reported £70,000 fee. He played in the North East until 1971.

Brian Hollinrake was on the Turf for the visit of the mighty Spurs. He recalls that even then, Spurs were acknowledged to be Burnley's great rival and had a high calibre side. "It was wonderful to watch Spurs and we had some great games with them that were a glorious advertisement for football. In the first half, Spurs were in control and went two up, but then McIlroy came into his own and we achieved a tremendous win. Many had been disappointed at Pilkington's departure, but Harris was quickly winning over the crowd."

It meant that the Clarets had taken three points from the new champions. Their meeting at White Hart Lane in December 1960 has gone down in the annals of Burnley FC as one of the greatest games. The Clarets had only just returned from midweek European Cup action when they faced the daunting task of confronting Spurs. The result was a 4-4 draw, but incredibly Burnley were four goals down before a tremendous fightback. Tommy Cummings says of the encounter: "It was as good a game as I ever played in during my footballing life. The standard of football that was played by both sides was unbelievable. With so many goals I suppose some might ask where the defenders were, but there could be no criticism of anybody, such was the quality. It was incredible and I'm sure for many of the players who took part it will be the best game they ever were part of."

The reigning champions found themselves trailing to a brace of goals by Cliff Jones and one apiece for Maurice Norman and Dave Mackay, on a muddy pitch hardly suited to the game of the season. Burnley appeared out of it, yet with half-time still not arrived there was the faintest glimmer of hope when McIlroy and Pilkington linked well and the finishing touch was provided by Connelly. In the second period, Robson and Pointer were on target and the scene was set for a magnificent finale. First both sides hit the post as they strived for the all-important goal – Spurs to again get a breathing space against their now relentless opponents, and the Clarets, of course, looking to bring themselves level. They did so when a one-two between Connelly and Robson saw the winger crash the ball into the far corner and the Spurs fans fell silent. There was still time for John White to miss a simple chance that would have robbed the visitors of the point they so justly deserved, but it was not to be and it was a happy Burnley contingent who began the long journey home.

This was the first season of the League Cup and, while many leading clubs opted not to enter in this inaugural year, Burnley were keen to take part. With hindsight it was probably a mistake. They reached the semi-finals, as they did in the FA Cup. But with European competition, it meant the team would play 62 games in the season and while, in theory, they had a large squad of 41 players, there was not the talent in the Reserves to adequately stand in for first-team regulars. In the early rounds of the League Cup, the second string were given an outing in a tactic that is echoed by Sir Alex Ferguson and Manchester United in the same competition today. With so much to play for, yet again Burnley would falter at the end of the season as both mental and physical fatigue set in.

In the new competition, Cardiff City were despatched with ease, 4-0, but in the next round, against Brentford, the reserve team could only manage a draw. A player who managed only six starts in the season got on the scoresheet. Andy Lochhead would soon become a much more regular figure on both the teamsheet and the scoresheet for Burnley. When Brentford returned for the replay, a more familiar-looking Burnley side triumphed 2-1. A 2-1 home win against Nottingham Forest and a comfortable victory at Southampton, by 4-2, booked the Clarets a place in the semi-finals and a date with their old rivals and Cup nemesis from the late Fifties, Aston Villa.

The club was warned for fielding an understrength team, but promptly did the same again in a League match against Chelsea, on the Saturday before the European Cup-tie with SV Hamburg, when only two first-team regulars, Cummings and Harris, turned out. Despite the game finishing 4-4, the club were fined £1,000 by the Football League Management Committee. Lord was to suggest that the penalty owed more to antipathy towards him on the committee than a fair reflection on Burnley's supposed misdemeanour.

The League Cup game against Villa was to prove another close-run thing with draws in both games in the two-legged fixture. The decider was played at Old Trafford and the winners would meet Second Division Rotherham United in the Final, but the fact the game attracted a crowd of less than 8,000 showed that the tournament had not yet caught the public imagination (and would not do so until the Final was moved to Wembley in 1967).

Five times Burnley would meet Aston Villa in the 1960-61 season – and they wouldn't win any of the games. Alex Elder and Jimmy McIlroy were away on international duty, but having fought back from 2-0 in the contest at Villa Park, and thus overcome the jinx of that particular ground, the Burnley players were confident. Villa scored first with a 70th-minute penalty after Adamson was penalised. Two minutes later the sides were level when Pointer set off on a run and crossed for Harris, who laid the ball on for Robson to score. With extra-time threatening, a speculative shot went into the net off a post and Villa were through. The semi-final was always going to be more of an attraction than the Final, and Burnley received praise from the competition organisers for participating and lending credibility to the tournament.

Elder had quickly cemented his position in the first-team squad since arriving as the youngest player in the championship-winning season, and had gained international recognition for Northern Ireland as well. His arrival at Turf Moor came about not through the club's talented scouts, though, but because of a Burnley spying mission that was initially directed at another player. In late 1958, Ray Pointer had still not convinced everyone that he was ready for first-team football and a party travelled to Belfast to watch a centre-forward playing for Glentoran. All eyes, though, centred on a 17-year-old full-back who displayed a maturity beyond his years and a wide range of skills. The Clarets had gone searching for a centre-forward and discovered a future international full-back. Elder was the only player to break into the team during the championship-winning season. His start in the first team could not have been tougher. He was assigned the task of marking Tom Finney in a derby game at Deepdale. Burnley lost 1-0, but Elder had done enough to show his potential. He won his first cap for Northern Ireland while still eighteen, against Wales in April 1960. He would win 33 more during his Burnley career and a further six after being transferred to Stoke City in 1967. The original task of the party sent to watch Glentoran had been overtaken by events. Pointer was quickly proving himself worthy of the number-nine jersey.

Dubbed 'the pocket blond bombshell' by the fans, for whom he was a great favourite, Pointer was another Burnley recruit from the North East, having been snapped up after he failed a trial at Blackpool. With an impressive goalscoring record of better than a goal in every two games, it was to be Bloomfield Road's loss. He scored 118 goals in 223 games for Burnley and was capped for England. Like many of this era, when he finished at the Clarets he made the short journey to Bury, although his Gigg Lane career was brief and he moved on to Coventry City before ending his career at Portsmouth. In Burnley's goalscoring records, only George Beel is ahead of him. He was to prove wrong, and in the most impressive fashion, those who doubted whether he would make it as a centre-forward at Turf Moor.

In the FA Cup, Burnley progressed confidently, beating Bournemouth, then Brighton and Hove Albion after a replay, before accounting for Swansea Town. In the sixth round their opponents were Sheffield Wednesday. Burnley travelled to Yorkshire and secured a goalless draw and then made no mistake on the Turf, winning 2-0 with goals from McIlroy and Robson. The team put behind them the pressures of a congested fixtures list and raised their game to give the lie to any suggestion that they might be tiring. To their undoubted skills was added some battling qualities as they comfortably accounted for Wednesday. Blacklaw in goal, who had been the hero at Sheffield, had little to do. In the 53rd minute, McIlroy went down the wing and his cross wasn't cleared by the defenders and in the scramble, Robson shot home. It was enough to bring youngsters on to the pitch and the police needed a few minutes to clear them. Fifteen minutes later, the game was safe when McIlroy was illegally stopped in the penalty box and the Irishman converted the penalty himself.

For Harold Gee, the replay was to have poignant memories. Then living and working in Manchester, he travelled to the game and met up with his father, who had travelled from Nelson. They watched the match together and celebrated a fine win for the Clarets. It was to be the last time he saw his father alive. "My father hadn't been well. He had a dodgy heart and I used to worry about him going on the Turf when there were big crowds. It was the last time I saw him, and watching Burnley was probably a fitting occasion."

The stage was set for yet another encounter with Tottenham Hotspur as the two finest teams in England again prepared to do battle. The venue for the encounter was the old bogey ground for the Clarets – Villa Park. Some fans went straight from Hamburg, where the midweek European Cup-tie had been played, to Birmingham for the FA Cup semi-final. They had been on a six-day journey and it wasn't over yet. What wouldn't today's Burnley fans give for that sort of itinerary? An estimated 3,000 fans travelled from Lancashire on special trains and all the coaches from miles around were hired. There were 70,000 at the game and the final scoreline of 3-0 to Spurs did not do Burnley justice. In the early exchanges, Burnley enjoyed the best of the play with McIlroy, as ever, orchestrating proceedings. Unfortunately, decisions were to go against them. Early in the second half, the Clarets had a goal disallowed for a push on Norman as Robson headed home. Later, the Burnley players claimed the ball was over the line after a goalmouth scramble, but the referee didn't give it. Spurs had got their first goal when a rare mistake by Adamson let in Bobby Smith. The same player got the second with a shot past an unsighted Blacklaw. By the time Cliff Jones scored in the 89th minute, it was all over.

The fixture congestion that had incensed Burnley and led to the £1,000 fine for fielding a largely reserve side against Chelsea on the week before the semi-final, was not to go away. There seemed some merit in the club's case, put forcibly by

Lord. Having already played two quarter-final matches against Sheffield Wednesday in March, the fixture list had involved a League game against Chelsea on Saturday, the 11th, the Hamburg European Cup game on the following Wednesday, and then the FA Cup semi-final against Spurs on the Saturday. To make the sense of injustice at the fine worse, the team against Chelsea had secured a 4-4 draw and it took a late Jimmy Greaves equaliser to prevent Burnley taking all the points. Such a programme certainly couldn't have helped Burnley's cause in two vital cup matches.

When Lord attended the Spurs celebration banquet at the Savoy Hotel in London later that year, he took the opportunity to call for some flexibility for teams playing in European tournaments as regards FA Cup and League fixtures. Present were many senior figures in football. What changes that were made could not help Burnley, who were ill-served by the game's rulers. The fact that even today, leading Premiership clubs are making the same complaints shows little action has been taken over the years.

Burnley had tried for everything with two domestic cup competitions, the League and the European Cup, and in a season that was memorable, although sometimes disappointing, they had lost the lot. How differently history would have viewed Burnley if they had succeeded. They came so close, only to ultimately fail. Lord, for one, did not begrudge Spurs their Double glory and believed the achievement would be a boost to English football and help encourage more fans through the turnstiles at a time of dwindling attendances. The Burnley players had also gained valuable experience and enhanced their reputations. Now they would try to emulate Spurs and win the Double.

Double or Nothing

I T WAS the 1961-62 season when this great Burnley side nearly gained football immortality for themselves. With the championship virtually assured, and a place in the FA Cup Final secured, the Double was on and the sense of anticipation in the town was unbelievable. The industrial mill town was poised to join Tottenham Hotspur as only the second team in the nineteenth century to achieve such a footballing landmark. Yet, as fans lament, two matches from the game's Holy Grail they faltered. The League title slipped from their grasp, to be gratefully grabbed by Alf Ramsey's Ipswich Town. And in a disappointing Cup Final, the Clarets lost to Spurs, their great rivals at this time.

Tommy Cummings believes that 1961-62 represented a tragedy for Burnley in many respects. The build-up to the Cup Final was undermined by a run of poor form in the League, which for much of the season Burnley had dominated. He believes the trip to Wembley ultimately cost the Clarets the championship. "In the back of their mind, every player wants to go to a Cup Final and play at Wembley and something about that must have preyed on our minds in the League. Ipswich came from nowhere to win the League, yet we were points ahead of them at one stage. I can only put it down to the lead-up to the Cup Final. I wasn't a player to shirk tackles, but there must have been others in the team where it happened."

Jimmy McIlroy recalls: "We threw the title away when we had it won. We were six points ahead with six games to play and had an awful run-in. I had picked up a thigh injury and wasn't fully fit and I think tiredness and injuries were a problem for some of the others. When things started to go wrong, we couldn't seem to turn it round."

The maximum wage had been abolished, but for now it had no affect. That would come later. The players were offered the new wage rates and all re-signed for the coming year. Indeed, Bob Lord had long advocated pay rises for professional footballers, even if he was opposed to removing the maximum wage. He felt that the earnings of footballers in the late Fifties and early Sixties had not kept pace with inflation and the professional footballer was, in real terms, worse off than his predecessors.

The League campaign started well. By the end of September, Burnley had lost only one of their opening eleven matches, although ominously it was a heavy 6-2 defeat against the team that would eventually lift the title, Ipswich Town. A fortnight earlier, the Clarets had beaten the same opponents 4-3 on the Turf, but it was to be a different story in the return fixture at Portman Road against a side that had only won promotion from Division Two the previous year. Within weeks, the First Division newcomers enjoyed a resounding win. They were also to prove this was no early-season flourish for a team newly-arrived in the top flight, before quickly sliding down the table. If the neutral view was that the Suffolk club would fade, and the experienced Burnley side would hold their nerve, it was to prove a false conclusion.

Early in the season, though, Burnley continued to notch up victories and, as in the two previous seasons, when they hit form it resulted in a landslide of goals: six in each of their games against Birmingham City, Leicester City, Manchester City and

West Ham United; and an incredible seven past Birmingham on their return. How the Midlanders must have cursed the sight of those claret and blue shirts.

After the trouncing of West Ham on March 3, Burnley were four points clear at the top of the table and had a game in hand on nearest rivals, Ipswich. Talk of the Double gripped the town. Donald Speak recalls: "They were hammering the goals in. The team was absolutely brilliant and I'll never know how we threw the title away. It wasn't a case of blaming any individuals, it just went so badly wrong. I'm sure some of them had Wembley on their minds and didn't want to miss out, but the League championship was ours for the taking."

Suddenly, with one hand already on the trophy, it all went horribly amiss as Burnley suffered a disastrous run-in to the end of the season. The old failing of being unable to maintain form to the bitter end had returned to haunt them again. From April they won only once in ten games to let the title slip. It was perhaps not a coincidence that the start of the poor form, with a goalless draw against Nottingham Forest, was the beginning of four matches McIlroy was to miss through injury. The town was numb as the ultimate honour was lost in a week-by-week torture which few could believe was unfolding. Always there was the thought that sooner, rather than later, the Burnley of old would emerge to make amends. But apart from a 2-0 home victory over Blackpool, it was not to be. That win, though, did feature a goal by Cummings – his first since January 1952 – and the Clarets were back on top of the League.

With two games of the season remaining, Burnley were two points behind the East Anglia side with a superior goal average. All was not yet lost, but they were never able to overhaul that deficit. Jack Cochrane remembers the delight in the Clarets' performance during the season turning into despair in the last five or six games when things started to slip from them. He said it was terrible to watch as a side that had been invincible a few weeks earlier, suddenly started letting easy points slip. Then he believes the players started to panic and were often playing for a draw rather than going for the win; their caution was the undoing of them.

Ambrose Allanson remembers the bitter disappointment of those closing matches in the title chase. Before the solitary Blackpool win, there had been three local derbies and the Clarets had failed to win any of them. A trip to Burnden Park when the pressure was on is never easy and there was no score. Then Manchester United came to the Turf and won convincingly 3-1. But the bitterest blow for Allanson was Blackburn winning by a single goal at Turf Moor. He felt that if the pressure had been maintained on Ipswich, the new boys may have cracked. Alas, with a home draw against Chelsea and a 4-0 defeat away to Sheffield Wednesday in those last two League games, there was no question of Burnley applying any pressure.

He added: "The fans kept working out what would happen if we won this match or that one, but then there would have to be a quick revision as we again failed to collect points. Looking back, though, it is amazing to think that Burnley were in the position of feeling they had thrown away a championship title. Those were the heights we had reached and, if we faltered at the last, there had still been some wonderful entertainment to savour along the way. We also had the Cup run to enjoy."

Indeed, there was still the FA Cup. It was with the enthusiastic support of all Burnley that the team set out for a match being dubbed the 'Final of the Decade', which pitted the two best teams of the day against each other, with the Clarets taking on a Spurs side that had done the Double the previous season. It was to be a disappointing day for the Lancashire club, and one that was to leave their much-respected side contemplating a season where they had threatened so much, yet had again ultimately fallen short at the last hurdle.

Burnley had reached Wembley by knocking out Queen's Park

Rangers, Leyton Orient, Everton, Sheffield United and, in the semi-final, Fulham at Filbert Street after a drawn game at Villa Park.

Brian Miller, like most professionals, believes that winning the League is the greater achievement and brings more satisfaction than a Cup Final success. However, with the title having slipped from Burnley's grasp, he was determined to enjoy the day at the Twin Towers. He said: "You need a bit of luck to win the Cup but, having got to Wembley, it was a great occasion and with the press and photographers you're the centre of attention during the build-up. Burnley and Spurs were the best sides in the League and everybody was expecting a great match. I remember seeing all our fans making their way along Wembley Way. The result went wrong for us, but one side has to win. Running out to be met by the wall of noise from a 100,000 crowd was a nerve-wracking experience, but our experience in the European Cup helped us. It was the last match of the season, but once the whistle blows and the game's under way it's just another game of football. You don't really notice the crowd then. Spurs had some good players and were virtually an international side. It was an even game and although we lost, the day itself was brilliant. You're very disappointed going up to get the losers' medal."

Harold Gee had travelled down in a family group in a VW Dormobile on the Friday night and stayed at relatives in Luton. He had acquired his ticket through Accrington Stanley, where he had a cousin who had contacts. Before the kick-off they had wandered into a café where they met a former player, Doug Winton, who had been full-back until Alex Elder broke into the side. With him was the then Rochdale manager Tony Collins and they signed Gee's programme as a souvenir. Inside Wembley he can remember the crush of the crowd and, along with the rest of the Burnley support, he was reasonably confident. "It was billed as the Cup Final of the Century and when we equalised, we thought it was going to be our day, but it was not to be. Afterwards we met a lot of relations for a party back in Luton. All

I wanted to do was to go to bed. I still go to bed by 9pm on a Saturday if we've lost, because I'm that disappointed."

Speak had also made the journey and enjoyed the brilliant atmosphere of the occasion, although the result was so disappointing. He thinks McIlroy had a poor game and the veteran Cummings was playing one game too many at the top flight. He was particularly exposed because he was up against a talented forward like England international Bobby Smith. He believes a better option would have been to switch Brian Miller to centre-half and bring somebody else in at wing-half but hindsight, as they say, is a wonderful thing. Yet he still has fond memories of Cummings, who had been a great servant of the club and, in his day, a popular and very effective centre-half.

The game itself got off to a bad start for the Clarets when inside three minutes, Spurs were ahead thanks to a Greaves goal. A long ball found Smith, who headed it on to Greaves and although Cummings appeared to have the danger covered, the Spurs man kept possession and his shot went in just inside the post. Burnley got on level terms in the 49th minute when Pointer robbed a defender and found Harris, who beat Baker and centred to Robson. His shot beat Brown. Barely had the cheers died down when Spurs restored their lead when White centred and Smith beat Miller to the ball and fired home. The decisive goal had an air of controversy about it. Cummings handled on the line and the penalty was awarded, but Burnley fans believe the referee should have stopped play earlier for a foul on goalkeeper Blacklaw by Jones. The linesman at first flagged, indicating he had seen the incident, but then put his flag down. Danny Blanchflower converted the penalty and Burnley's Cup dreams were shattered.

Cummings said: "The Wembley trip itself was a thrill. It's something that is very hard to explain. You know exactly where your family are near to the Royal Box and as I came out, I looked up and although I didn't really see them, it was wonderful to know they were there, taking everything in. Just walking out at Wembley for the Final is something you have to experience to understand. We were reckoned to be the two best teams in the country. When we conceded the opening goal so early I just thought, 'Oh hell.'"

When the final whistle sounded, all Cummings remembers is feeling pretty sick. "After going through so much in the previous month, it had all been shattered. All I wanted to do was go on my own and think. Everybody was saying we had done our best, but we didn't really play our best that day. Yet that normally happens in the Final. It is the occasion that gets to everybody. Even now, when I watch the FA Cup Final, I can sympathise with the lads on the losing side. I know what they are going through."

McIlroy had a somewhat controversial view of the Cup Final, describing it as 'the most disappointing Cup game I have played in from a footballing point of view'. He explained: "The Final lacked the atmosphere of every other Cup-tie I have played in. There was more atmosphere playing Bradford City two years earlier than in the Final itself. Wembley is such a wide, open arena and each club had only a small percentage of the tickets. It meant that far and away the greater percentage of the crowd were neutral. People in those days regarded a trip to the Cup Final as a social occasion."

He added: "As the two teams walked out, my old friend Danny Blanchflower, the Spurs captain, said to me: 'I bet you'll wonder what all the fuss is about.' He expressed what I had been thinking. From a players' point of view, all the hullabaloo between the semis and the Final puts you on cloud nine and you are not really adjusted to the game as you would be if it was a normal Saturday Cup game. I think it's why so many Cup Finals are disappointing. Our League games with Spurs were so enjoyable to watch and the crowds loved them, but by comparison the Final was somehow so flat."

McIlroy said the match itself was not a good game and nothing like the traditional clashes between the two teams. The early goal was a killer blow to Burnley's hopes. The Robson equaliser gave some hope. "If we could have kept it level for a few minutes, it might have developed into a good game, but they broke away and scored a second. The Burnley fans had hardly sat down from cheering our goal when Spurs were back in the lead. The result was sealed with the penalty. Danny was taking it and I was trying to signal to Blacklaw in goal which way he would hit it. Danny must have been aware of what I was doing because he turned to me and said: 'Do you want to take the bloody thing?'"

For a young Andy Lochhead, who had travelled with the squad as a reserve, it was a tremendous atmosphere. "It was wonderful to be involved, even as a reserve. Driving down Wembley Way and seeing the supporters in their colours was very emotional. It was good to have been there and taken part, but obviously everybody was down when we were beaten. I was to go back twice more with Leicester City and was on the losing end both times, so I know what its like."

As a season ticket holder, Ambrose Allanson had no trouble getting a Wembley ticket and travelled down to London on one of the many special trains laid on for the match. "We just didn't perform anything like we were capable of doing. There was just something missing. One or two key players were off form and although Robson scored the 100th goal at Wembley, at the end it was all very deflating. On the way down we were all in high spirits and it seemed as though the whole town had closed up for the day and come down to London. I think the fixtures towards the end of the season had started to pile up and that cost us dear in both the Cup and League. Players were getting tired. I think we had played so well that we deserved something at the end of the season, but you don't always get what you deserve in football."

Christine Marsden remembers watching the match on television with all the family crowded round, including her mum and gran who were not interested in football. It didn't matter because this was Burnley's big day and everybody in the town was behind the side, whether interested in football or not. When they lost, everybody was disappointed, but the team had done so much. She believes that it was the defeat at Wembley that really fired her interest in Burnley.

Brian Hollinrake had joined the RAF and watched the Final in a YMCA club in King's Lynn where he was the only Burnley supporter. The place was also missing any Spurs fans. Allied to the lack of any atmosphere was a game which he described as 'like a bad nightmare'. He added: "At the time I thought we played awful, but having seen it since, perhaps that's a bit harsh. In many ways I thought we were a bit unlucky, although McIlroy didn't look fit to me and Adamson and Cummings weren't getting any younger. Being in the RAF was to seriously limit my chances of watching Burnley for the next couple of years."

What made the night for McIlroy, despite his disappointment, was that at the Burnley dinner, where the comedian Tommy Cooper was the entertainer, the Spurs manager Bill Nicholson and Danny Blanchflower turned up. "Danny made a little speech praising the two clubs and congratulating Burnley on all they had achieved. I thought it was marvellous, a smashing gesture. I can't imagine it happening nowadays."

While the Footballer of the Year award was a great honour for Jimmy Adamson, particularly as he believed it was an award that belonged to the team as much as him personally, 1961-62 was ultimately a disappointing season as Burnley came so close and ended up with nothing. What was a particular blow was that it meant the club would not be in Europe the following season. Even in the early Sixties, he was clear that was where the future glories lay and was desperate for Burnley to be a part. Any hopes that the Clarets could go one better in both League and Cup, though, were destined not to be fulfilled. The revolution that would transform football over the next forty years would largely pass Burnley by. And contrary to Adamson's hopes, Burnley would not for much longer be part of the new international scene involving football.

Forward into Europe

EUROPEAN football arrived in Burnley in 1960-61 when as League champions it fell upon the Clarets to represent English football on the Continent. The small-town club did not let the nation down and their supporters were to be treated to some magical nights of football on the Turf. The European dream was to end in Hamburg in a nail-biting conclusion, but the final stages of the competition had been tantalisingly close. The Clarets would be reaching for their passports again in 1966-67 as a third-place finish in the League the season before gained them entry into the European Fairs Cup.

It was the European Cup, though, that sparked huge interest. The competition was still in its infancy, certainly as far as England was concerned. The nation's representatives up until then had been large city clubs, like Manchester United and Wolverhampton Wanderers. Where the big-name sides had been, Burnley were now to follow. Bob Lord, for one, was delighted that the club, having firmly established themselves on the domestic front, were now set to make a name for themselves across Europe.

For the players there was the responsibility of knowing they were representing not only English football, but the Lancashire town of Burnley. Jimmy McIlroy, an international who played in the 1958 World Cup, describes these European Cup games as the biggest he played in during his career. He recalls: "Being part of the Burnley team in Europe was almost frightening for me. No matter how big an international match was, I looked forward to it and didn't feel worried or nervous, but those European Cup nights with Burnley were the biggest games I played in. It was simply the fact that it dawned on me that here was this little town representing British football. It was such a tremendous task for us. We desperately wanted to put up a big show and I wasn't confident that we would. In the end they were memorable games for me."

A bye in the first round meant that Burnley's second-round opponents would be the French champions Reims, who boasted an impressive record both domestically and in the European Cup competition. In the previous ten seasons they had topped the French League four times and had twice been in the Cup Final. The calibre of their side was underlined with the presence of French internationals Raymond Kopa and Juste Fontaine. The latter had been the leading scorer in the 1958 World Cup but fortunately for Burnley he was missing through injury when the French side arrived for their match on 16 November, 1960.

A crowd of 36,742 were packed into Turf Moor for a game that had caught the imagination of the town. Among them was Brian Hollinrake who remembers: "It was something a bit different having the French in town. Instead of the usual Cockney and Brummie accents, there were French supporters with their flags. If Burnley was a culture shock for the London teams, I can't imagine what the place must have been like for those French players and fans as they made the descent into Burnley. For us it was wonderful. I remember McIlroy scoring, but it was not so much the game itself as the whole occasion that was special."

The French visitors had earmarked McIlroy as the danger and marked him tightly, but it merely left space for other players and

Burnley had an array of talent happy to take advantage. The chief beneficiary was to be Ray Pointer. Certainly, Reims were quickly made aware that this was a side to be reckoned with. Within a minute the Clarets had scored. A long pass by Miller was headed out by Rodzic but the clearance only went as far as Connelly. His ball forward found Robson who scored Burnley's first goal in European competition. After 22 minutes it was 2-0 when a McIlroy shot took a deflection that left goalkeeper Jacquet stranded. Burnley fully deserved their lead and McIlroy was to hit the post in the second half. Now it was on to Paris, where the Clarets knew they faced a difficult task against a French side that would be determined to gain revenge.

There was a hostile reception for the players well before the game started. As they walked out to inspect the pitch an hour before the kick-off, there were already around 40,000 French fans in their places and they greeted the Burnley party with not just chanting and abuse, but threw fireworks, oranges and bananas. When play got under way both sides produced good football.

A first-half goal by Robson appeared to have settled the issue. In the second half, though, Reims went all out to claw their way back into the game, roared on by their partisan crowd. It was in this cauldron, and after the French had been stealing yards at free-kicks, that manager Harry Potts walked on to the pitch to kick the ball back to the rightful place for a free-kick to be taken. He was ordered to the stand by the referee and was later fined by the Football Association and banned from the dug-out for the rest of the season. The French recovery was effectively ended by a marvellous goal by Robson. It was a solo effort with Robson collecting the ball in his own half and evading a series of tackles before his shot from 25 yards dipped into the net. Burnley may have lost the match 3-2, but they were through on aggregate, 4-3.

The German champions SV Hamburg were the formidable opposition in the next round as Burnley strove for a semi-final place against Barcelona. The Germans had dropped only one point in their domestic championship all season and arrived at Burnley in peak form. There had been a row over dates for the matches. Burnley stuck to their insistence on playing the opening fixture in January, away from FA Cup-ties. They had to accede, though, to a German request for the return in March, rather than February. On the opening meeting, Hamburg returned with their confidence dented after a 3-1 defeat. A late goal by outside-left Dorpel though was to prove crucial.

In Hamburg fears that a two-goal lead would not be enough were quickly confirmed. The German side were the better team on the night, but if the luck had been with the Clarets they could have gone through. The view of the players was that Burnley had as much of the play as Hamburg, but everything the Germans attempted came off. There was, though, no disguising the fact that the Germans were a fine team. The Lancashire club's defenders had no doubt as to the talent of Uwe Seeler, the Hamburg centre-forward, who after a disappointing display at Turf Moor that did not do him justice, returned to restore his reputation. The way the home fans carried him from the field showed the importance of his performance to the Hamburg cause on the night. The German side's manager, Guenther Mehlmann, accurately summed up the evening when he said: "We earned our victory, but we did have some luck with our finishing."

Hollinrake watched the return leg on television and can only remember the miss by McIlroy in the closing minutes, which would have tied the game on aggregate. The Germans were leading 4-1 on the night and 5-4 on aggregate when the ball fell to the Irishman. Hollinrake takes up the story: "He looked certain to score, but he hit the post. It took my breath away when he missed. It looked as though he just passed the ball on to the post. I remember it happening and we couldn't believe it. We were the width of a post away from going through. It was the second time in the match the woodwork denied McIlroy and the way the ball hit it second time round, I felt it was more likely that the ball would have deflected into the goal than come out."

Lord's view on European football after Burnley's travels to the Continent proved not just xenophobic, but also a long way wide of the mark, as the development of the game in Europe over the intervening thirty years has shown. In his book *My Fight For Football*, published in 1963, he said: "My summing up of Continental football is that they are marvellous winners, but damn bad losers. Their acts of sportsmanship are insincere; they play a scientific style of football, it's true, but when we employ similar methods – especially on Continental grounds – they resort to unfair tactics. We taught them to play football, but they have manufactured underhand, unsporting actions of their own. If the finest club teams in England met any Continental sides or Latin American sides under an efficient referee of strong character – a referee who stands no nonsense in any shape or form – I say that English football would come out on top nearly every time."

Burnley's travels had taken them not only into Europe, but also to North America. They had been invited to take part in a tournament in America and Canada aimed at promoting interest in football on the other side of the Atlantic. Other teams taking part included Bayern Munich, Sporting Club of Portugal and Sampdoria along with the Brazilian side, Bangu. Burnley had been invited before the title was won, but it was as champions that they set sail for New York. For many of the players the chance to see New York and travel on the liner *United States* was a wonderful experience. For the club and Lord it was a catalogue of disaster from start to finish and a public relations nightmare as well.

On the field, a game with Kilmarnock turned into a war as the Scots aimed to prevent the League champions playing any kind of meaningful football. Some of the games were played on pitches more often used for baseball and far from ideal for football. Off the field, the Burnley party had been unhappy with their hotel and had moved generating some hostile press back home. The arrangements were far from ideal and Lord was, not surprisingly, far from happy. He argued with the organisers, but little improvements happened. America, it seemed, was not yet ready for soccer. After Burnley's experience, Everton were to tread a similar path the following year and suffer similar problems. After that, the idea of a hearts and minds assault on the American sporting public was quietly shelved by the powers-that-be.

Third place in the League in 1965-66 provided one last passport into Europe before Burnley slipped into terminal decline. The Clarets set off for their European Fairs Cup-tie against VfB Stuttgart buoyed by an impressive run of form that saw them top the First Division. It must surely be the only time in Burnley's history that a fixture was arranged so that it did not clash with a beer festival, but they take such matters very seriously in Germany. Willie Irvine scored the goal that earned a valuable draw and made the Clarets clear favourites for the replay, but the sending off of Brian O'Neil was a blow. Predictions of a Clarets victory in the return leg were confirmed with a 2-0 win with Andy Lochhead and Ralph Coates grabbing the goals.

Next opponents were Lausanne-Sports and Lochhead has particularly fond memories of the match. It was not just the boat trip on Lake Geneva. Nor a vain search with Willie Irvine for a bar his colleague had found when he was in the city six months earlier. They never found it, but enjoyed a marathon tour of the city and a visit to a few sites. Rather, it was that he was lying on his bed on the afternoon before the game when George Bray knocked on the door to say there was a telegram for him. His wife had just given birth to a baby daughter. A goal against the Swiss was the perfect end to the day as Burnley won 3-1. When Lausanne returned to Turf Moor, the result was even more emphatic with a 5-0 win and the Scot getting a hat-trick

Then came the much sterner task of Italian opposition with a draw that pitted them against Napoli. In the opening encounter at Turf Moor, Lochhead remembers getting flattened by the Italian's centre-half, who then jumped on his head. He was sent off for his trouble, but threatened to kill the Scotsman in the return leg. Burnley humbled the star-studded visitors 3-0 and set up a return fixture that was to be dubbed 'The Battle of Naples'.

The hero of a 0-0 draw that ensured a passage through to the next round was goalkeeper Harry Thomson. He saved a penalty early on that could have changed the course of the game and then pulled off a string of fabulous saves to frustrate an increasingly desperate Italian side, who enjoyed the best of the play but could not find the Burnley net. The *Daily Express* christened the goalkeeper 'a God in a green jersey'.

If it had been a backs-against-the-wall struggle during the game, it was to continue to be so after the final whistle as, amidst disgraceful scenes, the players were attacked. Thomson had offered to shake hands with Orlando after the match, but the Italian spat in his face. Substitute goalkeeper Adam Blacklaw tried to intervene to prevent further trouble and around a dozen men, many members of the stadium staff, attacked him as the rest of the players ran for safety down the players' tunnel. The abuse and missiles hurled from the spectators during the game was bad enough, but this was too much.

Lochhead recalls: "It was one of the biggest stadiums I had played in and the dressing-room area was underneath and you went down steps at the side of the pitch. All hell broke loose after the final whistle with punches being thrown. The police came to get hold of Adam Blacklaw because an Italian had cracked his head at the bottom of some stairs. There was a glass panel in the door and it got smashed and Adam anchored himself with his arm through the broken pane to stop the police taking him away. The police had him by the hair and were trying to arrest him. Later they said it had been for his own safety and they let him go after half an hour. It was all a bit hairy. As we drove away from the stadium, we had to take the suitcases out of the boot and hold them against the windows of the coach because of the bricks and bottles. The police cleared the road for us and we went straight to the airport, on to the plane, and away. It was all quite exciting and a far cry from League football."

Tommy Henderson remembers Thomson coming into the local pub with the *Express* headline proclaiming him a 'god in a green jersey' and joking about it with a former Burnley 'keeper called Harry Atherton, who had played in the Reserves in the Forties. Holding up the paper Thomson said: "I bet they never said that about you." To which the veteran keeper replied: "True enough, but when it came over the tannoy that I was playing in goal, I used to hear people say, 'Oh Jesus Christ'."

Brian Lucas organised the transport for away matches for the supporters' club for many years and he remembers travelling with thirty other fans to see Burnley draw 1-1 with Eintracht Frankfurt in the first leg of the fourth-round tie in the 1966-67 Fairs Cup. The coach trip set off on Sunday and arrived on the Tuesday of the match. "It was very lively in the stadium and when we held out for a draw their fans started burning their flags because they thought they were going out. We were on a high because we thought we had done the hard part. We didn't have much time to see Frankfurt because we had to set off back straight away, but I remember thinking that we had really arrived as a club now we were playing Continental opposition. The main problem was getting threatened with the sack back at work because I had skipped off to go to Germany. Unfortunately, my picture appeared in the *Burnley Express* with a group of other fans. I'd been caught red-handed. It was worth it, though. Burnley were still one of the top sides in the country at that time."

For Lochhead, the return match was a frustrating time because Burnley should have gone through. He was also absent because of injury and was sorely missed. "We went to Germany and did all the hard work to get a draw and then got beat 2-1 at Turf Moor. It was a big disappointment for everybody. It was particularly bad for me because I didn't play in the game, having suffered a hamstring injury. After beating Napoli, there was a strong feeling among the players that we could go all the way. The Italians had been the tournament favourites. We weren't doing too well in the League, but success in Europe would have given everybody connected with the club a huge boost. We just didn't perform to our potential on the night. It was just one of those things."

On a personal note, a starring role in a European campaign, coupled with his goalscoring success in the League, had brought Andy Lochhead to the attention of richer clubs. The twists and turns of a footballer's life are many and if fate had dealt the cards differently, the Scot's career could have gone in a different, and more illustrious, direction. "The physio at Manchester City lived near to me and he made an approach asking if I was interested in going to Maine Road, because manager Joe Mercer was thinking of signing me. I went to see Mercer at his house and stuck a couple of pay slips in my top pocket because I was on £100 a week. He asked if I would like to play for City and I told him I'd love to. I went to show him the wage slips and he said, 'Don't bother taking it out of your pocket. You'll be on a lot more here.' An official approach was made to Burnley, but they wouldn't let me go. A year later they sold me to Leicester City and I reckon they lost about £100,000 on the deal. Manchester City went to Bolton and signed Francis Lee. The club were poised to take off and I could have been part of it with European football and a League championship. That's how lucky or unlucky you can be in football.

The Fairs Cup had generated great interest for the people of Burnley and been a great experience for the players, but the rounds were played against a disappointing domestic season in both the Cup and the League. The home attendances had also been disappointing and the hoped-for revenue failed to materialise. During the European matches, the largest home attendance was for the Eintracht Frankfurt game and that was only 25,161. Those who missed out would be disappointed if they hoped to see such fare on offer at Turf Moor in the future. For Burnley, the European dream was over, just as it was about to take an even greater grip on the public's imagination with Manchester United's European Cup triumph in 1968. Clarets fans can only wonder how the club would be viewed nationally today if they had triumphed in that European Cup showdown with SV Hamburg and gone on to become the first British champions of Europe.

Bob Lord

ONE man was synonymous with Burnley Football Club in the post-war years and he was neither player nor manager. As chairman from 1955 to 1981, Bob Lord was a controversial figure, a name known throughout football. No examination of Burnley in their glory years after World War Two and into the Sixties would be complete without devoting some space to the former barrow boy turned football club chairman. His aim was to put Burnley on the map and he achieved that during his tenure, even if the publicity was sometimes for all the wrong reasons. Love him or loath him, Bob Lord could not be ignored. His influence extended far beyond Burnley and he became the senior vice-president of the Football League and chairman of the FA Cup committee.

Even now in the town, the jury is still undecided on the man. Cynical dictator who used Burnley FC to raise his own profile and further his own ends? Or visionary who was gruff and spoke his mind, but whose heart was always claret and blue and who did all he could to ensure Burnley remained in the top flight? For most of his reign, he maintained his two great promises to the fans: the club would never slip below the Second Division, Burnley shares would always pay a dividend. Stories about the man who made his fortune from a chain of butcher's shops are legion. Almost twenty years after his death from cancer, former players and spectators are still telling them.

Certainly Lord never went out of his way to be popular. His comments were frequently ill-thought out and rebounded on him and Burnley FC. He got publicity for the club, but the old adage that all publicity is good publicity certainly does not always hold true. Among a wealth of faux pas perpetrated by Lord included a claim that Jews who ran television were trying to obtain soccer on the cheap. Then he said that Manchester people had too much sentiment about Manchester United after the Munich air disaster. Manchester United played like teddy boys in their violent approach to the game. And most players he knew couldn't run a chip shop, let alone a football club, and no more than ten per cent of them knew the laws of the game. When the criticism became too fierce, he would try to distance himself from the remarks, but never with too much success.

One way he responded to criticism was to blame the messenger. Journalists often incurred his wrath and he was quick to ban individuals and the titles they represented. Jack Cochrane got to know Lord through his involvement with Lowerhouse Cricket Club, where he was at one stage chairman. He remembers a Lancashire League knockout competition and Lord was approached by a young reporter asking for a comment on the game. "Piss off," was the reply from the Burnley FC chairman. Cochrane chided him for being discourteous when the reporter was only doing his job. He replied: "I'm sick and tired of reporters always on my neck." The journalist working for a local newspaper was David Davies, now the Football Association's executive director and one of the most powerful figures in English football.

However, nobody could accuse Lord of being half-hearted in his work at Burnley. He did not regard it as a position to enhance social standing and status. His supporters argue that without his forceful personality and hands-on approach, Burnley would not have survived in the First Division for as long as they did. It is said that Field Marshall Montgomery once asked him how Burnley, with a population of little more than 80,000, could achieve such prominence in football. Lord's reply was along the lines that it took qualities similar to those that overcame Panzer divisions.

He began in business with a horse-drawn cart, from which he sold meat. He bought out his boss at 19 and then landed a contract to supply the town's schools. He survived several court actions. The football club he oversaw became adept at discovering young talent, bringing out the best of them and then, with little thought for players or fans, selling them. His boast was that he never sold a player until there was somebody better in the Reserves. It some cases that proved the case, but by no means in all.

Brian Pilkington is a prime example of how the system worked. He is also a player who was unhappy at his treatment after a loyal and successful career with the club. Within a month of scoring two goals in the European Cup win against SV Hamburg in January 1961, he was on his way to Bolton Wanderers. In an interview with a Clarets supporters' website he described how the events unfolded. "I was transferred for no reason at all. I was in the first team, I was playing well, I was scoring and doing everything right. There were teams interested in me, including Preston North End, Everton, Blackpool and Bolton Wanderers. I had a choice where to go. Harry Potts called me into his office and said there was interest in me, and when I said I didn't want to go, he replied, 'The chairman's agreed terms.' I think it was that there was £30,000 offered. They had signed me for £10 from Leyland Motors and they'd had 300-odd League games out of me. In all my career at Burnley I was on £20 a week and so it's easy reckoning to say that I earned around £10,500 over ten years in wages. It meant after ten years' service they would have made a nice £20,000 and that wasn't bad money.

"I didn't want to leave, but they just said they had agreed terms. With hindsight I should have called Bob Lord's bluff and said. 'I'm not moving,' but at that time there wasn't the player power there is today. There was no freedom of contract. In those days they could just retain you and you could do nothing about it. They had Gordon Harris in the Reserves and he wasn't a bad player."

However, although Lord might have been autocratic, he was not conservative when it came to football. During the late Fifties and early Sixties, he attacked the establishment for failing to keep pace with evolution. He argued that nothing was done between 1920 and World War Two and would say that after the war there was stagnation for many years. He was never among the entrenched old guard of club directors opposed to every change. He supported the players' demands for higher wages, believing they had lost out in real terms since the war. He was professional in his approach and expected other football directors to do the same. He wanted professional football to be seen not as a dead end job, but as a career that brought good rewards and should attract the highest standard of recruits.

He joined the board in 1951 with the minimum 35 shares, and claimed he had been admitted by accident while the team was in Turkey. When through the various machinations of boardroom politics he became chairman, he quickly made a key change. It was the custom that each chairman was in office for three years before retiring to let another member of the Board have his turn. That was never going to be the way Lord operated. Once in, he was there to stay.

Jimmy McIlroy remembers that Bob Lord was the first to admit that his knowledge of football was not on a par with those who made their living playing and coaching the game. As such, he did not interfere in playing matters. It may seem obvious nowadays, but when he came to power, directors often wielded their authority in areas that would now be considered strictly the manager's preserve. An insight into how rivals operated is given by Tommy Banks, full-back for England and Bolton Wanderers.

He tells an anecdote that shows why Lord was so unusual in this respect. At Burnden Park, the directors had the last say on team selection and would frequently demand changes, particularly if the side was not doing well. He recalls one director, who played Sunday league football, was not adverse to sending notes on tactics at half-time to players who were internationals. And a story that underlines Lord's criticism of many of the League club directors in his day concerns a Bolton match at Preston North End where the Wanderers were being played off the park and Tom Finney was at his glorious best. A director sent a half-time note congratulating the team. He had failed to realise the Bolton players were in their change strip and the players in white were Preston, not his own club.

Ill-informed directors who regarded football as a social outing were not for Lord. As Jimmy McIlroy says, he was single-minded in his ambition to make Burnley FC a leading name in soccer. McIlroy found him an amazing character who could be blunt to the point of rudeness. Outbursts such as criticising Manchester United's team-building plans within a few days of the Munich air disaster succeeded in bringing widespread condemnation of Burnley from across the country. His outspoken manner ensured he made a lot of enemies. Another regrettable outburst was his anti-Semitic remarks at a dinner, when he underlined his opposition to too much soccer on television by saying: "We have to stand up against a move to get soccer on the cheap by the Jews who run television."

Lord was adamant that television was bad for football and that attendances would suffer. He felt television did not give enough for what it got. One wonders what his view would be now, with the astronomical figures being paid by television for the rights to screen more and more games. He particularly feared that live television would arrive, coupled with leading players as commentators, and that would be a big lure to keep the average fan in the armchair in front of the box, rather than going through the turnstiles. He might have had his faults, but he could be a pretty shrewd judge. The figure again is that forty million watched football live in the post-war years. Only half that pay to see the game today.

McIlroy adds: "He did much to bring about the transformation of the club. His skill for publicity meant that Burnley started to attract much media attention, although whether it was always positive was open to doubt. He set out to put the club on the football map during his period in office. It can certainly be said he did that."

While McIlroy's departure from Burnley was the saddest time in his playing career, and it was instigated by Lord, the Irishman does not hold it against him. Indeed, he says that up to that time he had got on well with the chairman. He adds: "I quickly learned that the secret with the chairman was never to challenge him or demand what you wanted. I remember that with the maximum wage limiting what we could earn from football, one way to make a bit extra was by writing a newspaper column. I went to him and said that I could do with a column, but said I knew it would be impossible playing for a little-town team like Burnley. I could see him bristle at that. By that weekend I had a column in the Irish edition of the *News of the World*. If I had gone to him and demanded he find me a column or I would consider moving where there was more opportunity to earn extra money, he would have shown me who was boss. He wouldn't have let me move and wouldn't have got me any newspaper work. You had to know how to approach him. By me saying that something was impossible because it was Burnley, he was determined to prove me wrong."

Brian Miller saw Bob Lord at first hand as both a player and on the coaching staff. He recalls: "Lord was a very controversial figure, but one thing about him was that he left the playing side to the manager and rarely interfered with the players. He did very well for us. When we won the League we went to the United

States and played in a tournament and we went on a Mediter-
ranean cruise. We always stopped at the best hotels. Selling
players is something he is criticised for, but it had to be done.
When the maximum wage finished, we were only a village club
compared with many of the other sides in Division One."

Tommy Cummings was already a first-team regular when the
controversial Lord arrived and he remembers a strong, stern
character who left nobody in any doubt that he was the boss. As
a butcher, Lord would occasionally bring some steak in for the
players, but apart from that during his playing days Cummings
had little to do with him.

It was when Cummings' playing days were over that Lord was
to play a big part in his career. He had moved to Mansfield Town
as player-manager in March 1963, but after eleven games he
retired from playing to concentrate on his managerial role. After
four years he was at a function in London when Lord approached
him and, in his typically gruff manner asked: "Do you want the
Villa job?" Not surprisingly, Cummings said he would be
interested in one of the biggest jobs in football. After all, who
wouldn't be? "Put in for it," was Lord's parting shot before
moving on.

Cummings adds: "It was a bit of a shock. I didn't have that
much experience and with hindsight I could probably have done
with a bit more. I got an interview and the date was during a
holiday in Newquay, Cornwall, so I travelled up to Birmingham
and was offered the job there and then. Bob Lord must have
suggested me. All I can say is that in the dealings I had with him,
I couldn't call him. I had only two years at Villa and, to be
honest, I wasn't ready for such a big club."

Andy Lochhead says that he always found the chairman a fair
man during his playing days until the time he left Turf Moor.
Then he discovered he wasn't fair at all. With the wage structure
starting to collapse, Lochhead, Brian O'Neil and Willie Morgan
were arguing that they should be on more money because they

contributed more to the team. Lord agreed to give the three an extra £20 a week. Within a few months, Lochhead was sold to Leicester City for £80,000, but he was still owed the £20 a week for the intervening time he had been playing at Burnley. When he asked the chairman, he was told: "Andy, that was verbal – and verbal doesn't mean anything. You're getting nowt." Yet he still believes Lord was a good man for the club and as much as anybody raised Burnley's profile. Burnley FC was in his heart.

Tommy Henderson was one of many who did not like Bob Lord. He remembers he was plotting behind the scenes long before he was chairman. In 1948, Harry Potts had refused to sign a new contract and was dropped before a League game against Arsenal. It was Lord who acted as the intermediary between board and player and who eventually brokered a deal within an hour or so of the kick-off. It was the machinations of Lord that Henderson was always wary of. On a lighter note, though, he remembers Lord used to sell meat to the players from a basket after training.

For the fans' view, Peter and Christine Marsden have found their opinion of Bob Lord changing over the years. Peter explained: "At the time, everybody disliked Lord. You could say we hated him. It is only as I've got older and seen how the club has gone downhill that I've come to realise he did a lot for Burnley and helped to keep us at the top, although we had started to go down while he was still in charge. He got everybody talking about Burnley and also Bob Lord. He must have been one of the first high profile chairmen. Now there are a few who are famous, but before Lord, the chairman was somebody the fans rarely ever heard of. Most chairman at that time just quietly got on with the job. That certainly wasn't Bob Lord's way."

Ambrose Allanson recalls: "I was in his company and I knew the man. A lot of people call Bob Lord and he was a hard businessman, but there was another side to his character. A friend of mine had a son with muscular dystrophy and he wrote to companies in Burnley asking if they could put a collection box in the works. The only reply he got was from Bob Lord, who also enclosed a donation. He was dogmatic. I remember he had a trick of taking his hearing aid out if he was losing an argument. I still think he was good for Burnley. Not so much on the playing side. The organisation at Turf Moor was so good at spotting and developing talent, my mum could have run that side of the club."

Cochrane, though, saw another side and admits he didn't like Lord. "He was an ignorant man and a bully. He wasn't a nice man at any time, but he could be worse. I remember he was a Freemason and used to play snooker at the Freemasons' Lodge on a Saturday. If it was an away game, he would send instructions that the table had to be vacated at 10pm so that he could play. On one occasion there was somebody on the table and he ordered a guy who used to work for him as a 'gopher' to get them off. Now when Lord played, the opponent always had to let him win. This evening the employee who had cleared the table on his instructions was obviously in no mood to give Lord a chance and when they played, he beat him easily. When he went into work on the Monday, his cards were waiting for him. Lord had sacked him."

Often, he believes, Lord's actions were not good for business or for Burnley. Selling McIlroy cost the club 5,000 spectators and could never be shown to be a good move. Cochrane recalls an FA Cup match against Bradford City in the championship-winning season. Burnley had earned a replay and as he was making his way to Turf Moor, Cochrane saw two little lads crying. When he asked what was wrong they said they couldn't get in because everybody had to pay full price. He paid for them to go in and later asked Lord why he had taken the decision that meant thousands of children were shut out because the junior entrance fee had been scrapped for the big game. His reply was that kids under fourteen shouldn't be going to football matches. "They should be at home doing their homework." Cochrane thought he was mad. Those children were the supporters of the future, but Lord was not bothered about that. He didn't have the vision to see beyond the next weekend.

When Lord was dying, he would be driven to the Lowerhouse Cricket Club ground and sit in the car watching the game. Members of the club committee would take it in turns to sit with him for ten minutes. As Cochrane says: "Ten minutes with Bob Lord was enough. When I talked to him, though, I was amazed how ignorant he was about football. He hadn't a clue. I went to his funeral and remember among the sombre-suited mourners, John Bond, the then manager, arrived wearing a white 'tropical' outfit. I had never seen anything so inappropriate. Bond was a disaster for the club as well. Later I used to go and look at Lord's grave. A friend of mine asked if I went to pay my respects. I told him no, I just wanted to make sure he hadn't got up again."

The Beginning of the End

BURNLEY were to last at the top level longer than any of the other Lancashire mill town clubs largely because the system that had brought the Clarets to power was still in place. Events, though, were making it increasingly difficult to compete with the big-money clubs. Many fans believe the beginning of the end came with the selling of Jimmy McIlroy in 1963. Rather, though, the sale came at a time when the writing was already on the wall. The abolition of the maximum wage, freedom of contract for players and rapidly rising transfer fees all played their part in the inexorable decline.

A small town like Burnley, no matter the loyalty of its support, just could not command the average attendances needed to compete with city clubs with deep pockets and a huge population to tap into for support. Indeed, Burnley had never been major players in the transfer market. For one thing, the idea was anathema to chairman Bob Lord. They might have sold, but they rarely paid out large fees. The scouting system and their in-house training programme had, for the best part of two decades, been a conveyor belt for talent. When there was a hiccup in the quality coming through, it presaged problems. While other clubs in East Lancashire succumbed earlier, Burnley were able to keep their

First Division status throughout the decade and taste European competition once more in 1966-67.

Lord's vision for Turf Moor also proved a financial burden which the club could have done without. Unwilling to pay large fees for players, he still managed to have grandiose plans for the ground and its facilities. In fairness, it was part of a commendable belief that football could only continue to command a large audience if it provided modern, attractive stadiums for the fans. It would, he believed, be a more efficient way of pleasing the supporters than buying star players at huge prices. In the early Sixties, plans were unveiled for a new stand for the Bee Hole End and Brunshaw Road side of the ground. It would seat 17,000 and cost £200,000, which Lord hoped to fund from the club's profits.

On the field, the decline was gradual at first. Burnley finished a creditable third in 1962-63 and then ninth the following season. By 1964 they were twelfth but the following year back in Europe, thanks to a third place. That season was to be the high water mark for the club in the late Sixties and beyond. Thereafter it was fourteenth for four seasons, prompting the jibe that Burnley were the fourteenth-best team in the country. Soon, being fourteenth in the First Division would have been enough for the fans.

Burnley have always had to sell and with attendances falling and the transfer market spiralling out of control, it was inevitable that the club would have to part with players, although the Midas touch of having talented newcomers waiting in the wings was still not quite deserting them. One player who had signed for Burnley in 1958, from the Renfrew club in Paisley, was to give yeoman service from 1962-63 season when he broke into the first team, taking over Ray Pointer's number-nine shirt, with the blond bombshell moving to inside-right. Andy Lochhead would become the sixth Burnley player to score a century of goals for the club and holds the unique record of twice scoring five goals in a game. After both Pointer and Jimmy Robson left the club, Lochhead teamed up with Willie Irvine in a devastating partnership during the mid-Sixties. Lochhead won an Under-23 cap for Scotland in 1963, but full international honours eluded him. He was sold to Leicester City in 1968.

Willie Irvine was another who showed that the Burnley system was still working. He had joined the Clarets as a junior in 1960 and broke into the first team as a regular in 1964-65 when he replaced Robson. His scoring prowess was quickly brought home to the fans when, in only his second game for the club, in 1963, he scored a hat-trick in a 3-1 victory over Birmingham City at Turf Moor on the last day of the season. His partnership with Lochhead was feared throughout the League and the two scored 118 goals between them in the three seasons from 1964-65. His career suffered a setback with an injury in which he suffered a broken leg and shortly after he moved to Preston North End in March 1968. He was to also play for Brighton and Hove Albion and Halifax Town before retiring in 1973.

Lochhead recalls playing for Burnley during the Sixties after the heyday was over. "We always finished about half-way, but we never really challenged for the League. We weren't at the top, but we were still very near it. We could hold our own and the team I joined played well as a unit. We didn't have any stars or outstanding players, but we worked hard for each other. That was reflected with everybody being on the same money, despite the maximum wage having been abolished. We got £60 plus £40 appearance money and win bonuses."

Yet Lochhead was nearly lost to Burnley, as the player himself explains. He had been for a trial at Sunderland, but failed the medical because of a hernia problem. Burnley were not deterred and after a week's trial offered the 17-year-old a twelve- month contract on £8 a week. As was typical in those days, he had to serve a long apprenticeship before breaking into the first team four years later. He played in a successful Central League side that could attract crowds into five figures.

"When I arrived I was very naïve," he recalls. "I hardly knew where Burnley was, but I had heard of the place through the football team. I was happy to be away from Clydebank and Glasgow and to be given a chance in football. It was good to be away from the religious divide that exists in Glasgow. All my family were Orangemen and my brothers got into fights because of it. I never got involved and was glad to be out of that environment. Burnley was very different and the Sixties were a great time to be playing football. The standard was superb and there were world-class players performing at Turf Moor as the best teams in the land came to play us."

Another player who emerged in this era was Brian O'Neil, and the old trainer George Bray rates him on a par with any who came from the North East after being discovered by the legendary scout Jack Hickson. The only problem for Bray was that O'Neil liked a drink. He explained: "He was one of the finest players to come from the North East – and Burnley had a good few – and on a Saturday he could do the stuff, but Friday nights used to be a nightmare. Having a drink in itself was not a problem because you could get the player down to the training ground and sweat it out of them. I had to do a lot of that with Brian. Yet come a Saturday it never showed and he always gave 100 per cent for ninety minutes. He was a great character and you couldn't meet a nicer lad."

O'Neil was a tough midfielder who was always popular with the fans. He arrived as a junior in 1960 and three years later had the daunting task of replacing Jimmy Adamson. The styles of the two players differed greatly, with the former the more cerebral and the later the hard battler, but both proved effective. O'Neil was a regular for seven seasons and never gave less than 100 per cent. He may not have had Adamson's football brain or finely tuned skills, but he made up for it with maximum effort and a desire to get stuck in. It was an attitude they loved on the terraces. He moved to Southampton at the end of the 1969-70 season for £75,000. Two years later, the final move of his professional playing career saw him go to Huddersfield Town.

Lochhead has his own memories of the veteran club man Bray, who was his trainer. At this time the trainer had no coaching role as such, but was responsible for the fitness of the players. And unlike modern-day training regimes that are geared to the individual needs of the player and designed to improve everything from upper body strength, to sprinting skills to stamina, the training offered by Bray was much more basic. Lochhead said: "Basically, George just ran you until you spewed up. He would do things like having you run so many sprints in so many seconds and would time you on his watch. It was years later that I discovered the watch didn't even have a second hand on it."

It was the 1962-63 season that saw Lochhead firmly established in the first team. He remembers a third-round Cup draw that pitted the Clarets against the team that had beaten them in the previous season's Final, Tottenham Hotspur. "It was January and snowing and the game had been cancelled once and when it went ahead, there was a covering of snow on the pitch. For the players who had been at Wembley the previous year, there was a point to prove. There was also a determination to get back to Wembley and this time win the Cup. Before the game Bob Lord had us all in the boardroom and told us we were on £100 a man to win the game and every other round of the Cup. I would have run through a brick wall for £100. It was a good Spurs side, but we beat them 3-0. I can remember the goal I scored. Harris cut the ball back from the left wing and I hit it with my left foot and it went straight into the top corner. Our run, though, didn't last beyond the next round. We played Liverpool and it went to a replay at Anfield. With the clock ticking down, Blacklaw kicked the ball against Ian St John and then pulled him down and Ronnie Moran scored the penalty and that was it."

The replay, though, is remembered more for what happened afterwards than the events on the pitch. It proved to be Jimmy McIlroy's last game before he was transferred to Stoke City. The young Lochhead, newly-arrived in the first team, recalls: "I had no idea what was going on. We knew there was a bust up between him and Lord. There was sadness in the dressing-room. Time has proved that he was probably Burnley's best-ever player. He certainly made my job as a striker easier with the service he provided. His ability to deliver the ball was superb. He had a lot of natural talent and was a real crowd pleaser."

In the 1963-64 season Burnley finished ninth in the League and narrowly lost 3-2 to West Ham United at Upton Park in the sixth round of the FA Cup after having disposed of lower league opposition in the shape of Rotherham United, Newport County and Huddersfield Town. There were still, though, performances that stirred echoes of the near-invincible Clarets side of just a couple of seasons earlier. Keen fan Brian Lucas remembers an epic encounter against Spurs at the end of the season that ended 7-2. "It was one of those games when everything just clicked. Spurs were still one of our great rivals and to see them played off the park like that was wonderful. When they peaked, Burnley could rattle up some big scores against the best."

Peter Marsden's memory from the season was a Boxing Day encounter with Manchester United on the Turf in which the Clarets triumphed 6-1. "I didn't like Manchester United in those days and I still don't and it was always special to see us hand out a beating. United were a club with money then, just as they are today, but we were always a match for them in the Sixties." Sadly for Burnley fans, when the teams met at Old Trafford two days later, it was United's turn to run riot and they won 5-1. Lochhead, who had scored four against United on Boxing Day, again weighed in with Burnley's only goal of the return match. Burnley ended that season with a 7-2 home win over Tottenham.

The 1964-65 season was a mediocre one for Burnley, who finished twelfth in Division One. It had started badly with the side going eight matches without a win until a 3-2 victory over West Ham. There was no glory on the Cup trail as they went out to Manchester United, 2-1 at Old Trafford in the fifth round. Yet although the final League position was nothing remarkable, and as the campaign drew to a close there was nothing to play for, Brian Hollinrake remembers the last game of the season because of the controversy which surrounded it. Chelsea were the visitors and manager Tommy Docherty sent most of his players home as a disciplinary measure. "They had been on the pop or something and had misbehaved. It made for a terrific end to the season with Andy Lochhead getting five goals and Willie Irvine also bagged one. Willie Morgan just kept hitting centres over and the defenders couldn't cope. Burnley were no longer the great side we had been, though, and the signs were there that we were on the slide. The Chelsea game was a glorious reminder of the past. It had been rumoured that the Chelsea players who had been disciplined weren't going to go home and would watch the match from the terraces, so it was flattering when a reporter came up to me and asked if I was a Chelsea player. I did play quite a bit of football in the RAF, but not to that standard."

Brian Lucas also has happy memories of the match. One of the stewards allowed him to sit on a turnstile to see the game. Within five minutes, Burnley were 2-0 up and the youngster relayed the news to the people still queuing to get in. "I told one bloke that we were 2-0 up and he didn't believe me. He just told me to stop joking with him. It was an incredible game and a real reminder of when we were at our best, even though Chelsea were missing a lot of their team because they were suspended."

A sign of the times behind the scenes was that for only the third time since the war, the club reported a financial loss on the year up to March 1964. Although it was only £7,881, and the deficit was quickly overcome with the sale of John Connelly to Manchester United, it was a sign of the financial pressures that were to come. The wage bill was rising and players were beginning to flex their bargaining muscles. Alex Elder asked for a pay rise and to be put on the transfer list, which the club refused and he eventually stayed. Plans to build the new stand were quietly put on the backburner.

After the disappointment of the previous year, on the playing front the 1965-66 season was to make amends. It was to be Burnley's last great hurrah and provide one last chance of European football. Elder was appointed club captain and two wins and two draws in the opening fixtures saw Burnley top of the First Division. When Irvine scored in a 1-1 draw with Leeds United, it marked the start of a goalscoring run that saw him hit the back of the net in seven consecutive League games, equalling a record established by Ray Pointer.

Another Burnley hero who emerged in the mid-Sixties was to collect a rather more unwanted record when the old enemy, Blackburn Rovers, were the opponents on New Year's Day 1966. Willie Morgan became only the fifth Burnley player to be sent off. He got his marching orders after aiming a kick at Rovers centre-half Mike England in what was an ill-tempered match. Burnley won 2-0 to keep them second in the League behind Liverpool. Morgan was spotted by scouts for the Clarets in his native Glasgow and joined the club at seventeen. A right winger, he replaced John Connelly and was eventually to again follow in Connelly's footsteps when he also joined the playing staff at Old Trafford in the summer of 1968. A Scotland international, he returned to Burnley in the 1975-76 season as the Clarets strove to head off relegation. He played only twelve games before moving on to neighbouring Bolton Wanderers, where he stayed for five years. He played in the United States and had a spell at Blackpool before retiring in 1982.

In the FA Cup, Lochhead scored five goals in a 7-0 demolition of Bournemouth in a replay at Turf Moor after Burnley had travelled to the south coast and earned a 1-1 draw. It was to be Spurs in the next round and another thriller. There were seven goals, but the vital one went to Alan Gilzean, whose strike in the 88th minute saw the Londoners edge victory. Cochrane recalls: "It was remarkable how often the two clubs' paths crossed so much in the early Sixties and they were usually great games. Unfortunately, the Spurs seemed to edge too many of them on the big occasions for my liking."

In the League, Burnley had trailed Liverpool for most of the campaign and when they were the visitors to Turf Moor on April 23, the Merseysiders needed only a point to clinch the title. They didn't get it as Burnley won 2-0 with goals for Irvine and Ralph Coates. The Clarets missed out on the runners-up spot on goal-average, though, thanks to a home defeat against Leeds United, which enabled the Yorkshire club to squeeze just ahead of them. The match featured one goal and it was a bizarre one. When it seemed impossible, Elder managed to lob the ball over Blacklaw for an own-goal from the most acute of angles.

Coates was another of the new generation of stars coming through at Turf Moor. Yet another player to make the journey from the North East, Coates was an attacking midfielder who joined Burnley in 1962 as a sixteen-year-old. An England international, he went to the World Cup finals in Mexico in 1970. After more than 200 games he was sold to Spurs in 1971 for £200,000, where his career prospered.

At the end of the season Ambrose Allanson recalls: "We knew that the title was lost, but it was good to see us put one over on Liverpool. It was like the early Sixties again as we were taking on and beating the best in the League. We had some good new players coming through and the feeling was that if we could keep the squad together, then we could be back to our old best. Sadly, it didn't happen."

The Legacy and the Future

WITH promotion to Division One in the first season of the new millennium, there was a buzz about Burnley FC in the old mill town. Within weeks of the 1999-2000 season ending, the club had sold more than 10,000 season tickets for the coming campaign. While those of a more cautious nature hope for a couple of years of consolidation, the more optimistic are already casting envious eyes at the Premiership. If the likes of Bradford City can do it, why not Burnley they argue.

Jimmy McIlroy is delighted for both the club and its fans, who have had to contend with some lean times in recent years and yet have still remained loyal. His pride and a fear that he would be labelled a scrounger meant he never rang to ask for a free ticket, but on one Saturday a decade ago he accompanied his son to a game when Burnley were in the old Fourth Division and they stood behind the goal, ironically at what is now the site of the recently opened McIlroy Stand.

He said: "I was in the queue for the turnstile when I saw the sign saying entrance £5. I was amazed to be paying that to stand behind the goal and watch Fourth Division football. When I got back, my wife pulled out a 1960 stand season ticket that cost £5. I know regarding prices I was still living in the past, but it is a measure of the support that the fans continued to spend their hard-earned money watching Burnley, even in the worst times."

McIlroy counsels against getting too ambitious for the future too soon. Promotion, he believes, is a dream that can quickly turn into a nightmare as clubs are forced to spend to stay at the higher level. Frequently they fail and it can bring financial ruin. He hopes that Burnley can now maintain a respectable place in Division One, which should keep the majority of fans happy. A place in the play-offs would be a bonus. The chance of some derby games against the likes of Bolton Wanderers, Preston North End and Blackburn Rovers is a reality that can be savoured and will revive old memories.

Andy Lochhead takes a similar view of Burnley's hopes for the future. On Saturday home games he works at the club, greeting the sponsors and giving them a tour of the ground with a few anecdotes from the good old days thrown in. The veteran player is impressed with the set-up now at Burnley. There is a ground he regards as second to none and training facilities with which any young players would be delighted. The signing of Ian Wright, and his effect on the attendance, showed that the crowds are still there and ready to support the Clarets. "I think Burnley have a long way to go to get back to where we were. Now we have got into the First Division we will need four or five new players. The Premiership is certainly a long way off and we need to take things step by step."

Since the heady days of the League championship win, there has been a spiral of decline. Brian Miller has seen most of it as part of the backroom staff or in the manager's chair himself. There were the four seasons at the end of the Sixties when Burnley made the fourteenth spot in the League their own. Then the first season with Jimmy Adamson in charge and the quote that came to haunt him that Burnley would be 'the team of the Seventies'. By the end of that season, the idea of being fourteenth in the League's top flight is something the Clarets fans would have greedily grasped as they found themselves relegated. They got back into that top flight, but 1975-76 was to be their last time among the elite as they faced relegation again. As the team slid down the divisions, Miller was to savour glory and despair. He was the manager who took Burnley back into the Second Division as champions of the Third. He was then famously in charge for the 'Orient Game'. The picture of him peering anxiously from the dug-out during the tense closing minutes is a famous image in the town. It was the final match in the 1986-87 season which Burnley needed to win against Leyton Orient to stay in the Football League.

Miller's unique experience gives a cautionary tale in these times of rocketing finances in running a football club. He said: "I remember being told at one stage not to buy any boots because we couldn't afford them. What were the players supposed to wear? Then we had to ask the bank manager if we could take on two players on free transfers. There was no fee to pay, but we needed permission to make sure we could afford the extra wages. At the lowest point, Burnley were very short of money and for the future they need to plan carefully. Everyone knows that nowadays it is all about money and very few professional football clubs make any."

Looking back on his own playing days he adds: "When we were playing at our height, I don't think at times we realised how good we were. We took it for granted. We had Jimmy McIlroy, who was the outstanding player, but there were around eight or nine internationals in the side. We weren't frightened of anybody and if we hit form, then we could destroy sides. Along with Spurs we were the best sides and they probably had the edge. They certainly got the publicity. We were the lads from a little town up north. Whether Burnley can ever get back to that level is difficult to predict, but I certainly hope so. The problem is that with every year that passes, the gulf between the Premiership and Division One gets wider, and more and more of the best players in Europe keep arriving. It is hard to imagine Burnley being in a position to bid for leading Continental players at the prices they fetch and the wages they demand. It makes it all the harder for the club to get back. The new board are trying to sort out the finances. But will it be enough?"

After an association of more than forty years with the club, Miller still enjoys going to watch the team and has happy memories of his time as player, coach and manager. The players from the Sixties era had not officially got together until recently, but the opening of the Jimmy McIlroy Stand and the fortieth anniversary of the League championship win saw them reunited and there was the chance to swap memories and wonder whether in another fifty years Burnley players would be meeting up to celebrate similar triumphs.

Alastair Campbell is one of a generation of Burnley fans who have distant, hazy memories of the glory days, but the reality since is far more fresh in the mind. It has not, though, dented his lifelong commitment to the club or undermined the belief of a lifetime that the Clarets will return to their rightful place among the game's top teams.

He said: "Looking back, there's no point denying the disappointments outweigh the moments of magic. When I was three, Burnley were League champions. The year I first saw them, aged five, we were two games away from winning the Double. I followed them from the very top to the very bottom. By the time I was 29, in 1987, we had to win 'The Orient Game' to stay in the League, a spectacular fall, victory that day was as momentous in its way as those that had given us our two League championships and our 1914 FA Cup triumph. Having survived, every Burnley fan is convinced that although it's now a quarter of a century since we left the top flight, one day we'll be back."

The passion in the town, he believes, was reborn with the game against Leyton Orient, when the community woke up to the significance of what it was they nearly lost. Promotion to

Division One and the rush for season tickets within weeks of the season closing, as fans prepared for the new campaign in the higher division, underlines the new devotion. Now Campbell and fellow fans hope that, in his words: "The ghastliness of years spent traipsing around uncovered away ends, being patronised in programme notes – 'great tradition, but you're crap,' was the general message – may be over for good."

Certainly Tommy Cummings is confident that glory days are just around the corner for the club he represented with such distinction. He retains his links with Turf Moor, working on match days welcoming corporate guests and telling tales of Burnley's great days. "It's fabulous to talk to people because everybody is so keen for Burnley to do well. Everybody at the club knows that, and they are just as keen. The new directors are committed to getting the Clarets back where they belong. I don't know how soon it will happen, but I am sure Burnley will be back playing in the Premiership. They might not be with the top four or five clubs, but being in the same division will bring the leading teams back to Turf Moor – and that is a prospect to relish."

Brian Hollinrake had his passion for Burnley restored with the infamous Orient game. After years away with the RAF, he had trained as a teacher and was working in the Isle of Man. He went jogging, listening to the live match report on the radio as he went. "We were 2-0 up and I was just about to turn for home when Orient scored, and it was so tense I had to keep running to alleviate the trauma in my mind. At one point I knew that with seven minutes left I would be at the sea terminal by then and it would be over. We would have survived or gone. When the final whistle went, I leapt in the air and people walking on the seafront looked at me as though I was some kind of maniac. It was then I realised my five-mile run had turned into a 20-mile plus marathon and I was shattered. I hadn't felt a thing until the final whistle went. I then realised how close we had come to losing our heritage. After that, going round the Fourth Division grounds supporting them was like some sort of penance. But then there has been the euphoria of climbing back. If Bradford City can make it into the Premiership, so can we."

Peter and Christine Marsden looked forward to Division One football and the derby matches that the fixture list threw up with Preston North End, Bolton Wanderers and Blackburn Rovers all visiting Turf Moor in 2000-2001. Christine teaches in a local school and on the eve of the season she said: "The talk in the playground now is all about Burnley FC. Winning promotion has really caught the kids' imagination. I would say 95 per cent of those interested in soccer are Burnley fans. They have never known anything other than the bottom two divisions so they are savouring the success and there is a real buzz about the football club in the town. They wear their Burnley football shirts and are proud of the team."

On the field, the couple think that consolidation will be the key for the next two seasons, with perhaps a good Cup run or two to bring excitement back to the stadium. They point out that other small-town clubs have made it into the Premiership and stayed there, so Burnley should be able to do the same. The board is a forward-thinking one and the support is returning to ensure a healthy revenue. "When the team is successful, it is good for the town and gives everybody a lift. People of our generation and older, saw a lot of success. We've stayed loyal because there's no way you can just start supporting somebody else. Now the youngsters want a successful team to follow. We've had the bad days, we are ready for the good days to return and we can enjoy some good memories."

Ambrose Allanson still has his season ticket and enjoys his days out at Turf Moor, although not as much as in Burnley's heyday. He recognises the game has changed a great deal in the time he has been following the Clarets. The wages which players can earn nowadays and the lack of the loyalty to their clubs appals him. "Commitment and loyalty have gone out of the game. Players are prepared to hold clubs to ransom, and even with some of our players, you know that if they don't get the terms they are happy with, then they will go. The finances in the game make it hard for small-town clubs like Burnley to compete."

He also thinks that some of the camaraderie has gone from the game, certainly among spectators. In these days of segregation, friendly chats with opposition supporters about the merits of players on either side are a thing of the past. But also he thinks that a spirit of fellowship has disappeared among the players. He remembers Burnley playing Bradford City and Ray Pointer had just been capped for England. Before the match the Bradford centre-forward walked over and shook Pointer's hand and congratulated him on winning his England cap. A fellow pro wishing another player well is not something he believes would be seen today. In general, for all their money the players set a poor example in the way they conduct themselves, he feels. They have become more like film stars than sportsmen and have lost touch with the man in the street.

He was there for the Orient game when Burnley nearly slipped out of the League. If that had happened, he believes it would have been for good. Burnley would have gone the way of their near-neighbours Accrington Stanley, whose demise was ironically hastened by Bob Lord, who having been called in to advise on the club's finances, concluded they would gain more in the Lancashire Combination than in the Football League. The old chairman would have been turning in his grave at the idea of Burnley being a game away from football oblivion.

Allanson, though, thinks that having put such setbacks behind them for good, the only way now is up. He is another who thinks the Premiership beckons. Nobody can knock the optimism of the Clarets fans in the town. He argues: "The set-up is in place and success breeds success and we have started to enjoy some of that. I think someone will put money into the club to enable us to compete. There is something about Burnley that excites passions and if we can get a good run, the support will come flocking in, not just from the town but the whole of the Rossendale Valley and out as far as Yorkshire. It's a different world at Turf Moor now compared with a few seasons ago. They are geared up for the job and are committed to bringing success back to Burnley FC. There is a firm foundation."

After watching Burnley for the best part of eighty years, Jack Cochrane is happy with the club's fortunes at the moment. This is a man who was caned at school for playing truant in 1927 to watch the only international staged at Turf Moor, when Burnley players Louis Page and Jack Hill were picked for the side to guarantee a good turnout. England lost 2-1 against Wales and Hill scored an own-goal. Cochrane believes Burnley have woken up to the fact that the fans do matter and they will support the club if they are given something to cheer. "Bob Lord never cared about the fans and neither did his successors, but I think the present regime do. Everybody knows that nowadays a football club cannot be run on the gates alone and the commercial side has to be right. That is happening and is welcome. But innovations like reduced fees for children are helping to ensure another generation of Clarets fans is coming through. It will be a year or two before we are back in the Premiership, but we will get there."

The last word goes to Alastair Campbell who says: "I look at today's kids, millions of them who support Manchester United, and pity them. The vast majority never get to see them play. And, as their team has recently won everything – including the Champions' League – in the most breathtaking manner imaginable, all they have got ahead of them is disappointment Those of us reared on disappointment will have far more truly magical moments in sport than those raised to expect that every game and every trophy is a piece of cake. For young United fans, the only way is down and, believe me, it's a hellish journey to make."

Index